Your Future Face

Your Future Face

The Customized Plan to
Look Younger at Any Age

DENNIS GROSS, M.D.,
with Cara Kagan

VIKING

VIKING
Published by the Penguin Group
Penguin Group (USA) Inc., 375 Hudson Street, New York, New York 10014, U.S.A.
Penguin Group (Canada), 10 Alcorn Avenue, Toronto, Ontario, Canada M4V 3B2
(a division of Pearson Penguin Canada Inc.)
Penguin Book Ltd, 80 Strand, London WC2R 0RL, England
Penguin Ireland, 25 St. Stephen's Green, Dublin 2, Ireland
(a division of Penguin Books Ltd)
Penguin Books Australia Ltd, 250 Camberwell Road, Camberwell, Victoria 3124, Australia
(a division of Pearson Australia Group Pty Ltd)
Penguin Books India Pvt Ltd, 11 Community Centre, Panchsheel Park,
New Delhi - 110 017, India
Penguin Group (NZ), Cnr Airborne and Rosedale Roads, Albany, Auckland 1310, New Zealand
(a division of Pearson New Zealand Ltd)
Penguin Books (South Africa) (Pty) Ltd, 24 Sturdee Avenue,
Rosebank, Johannesburg 2196, South Africa

Penguin Books Ltd, Registered Offices: 80 Strand, London WC2R 0RL, England

PUBLISHER'S NOTE: Every effort has been made to ensure that the information contained in this book is complete and accurate. However, neither the publisher nor the author is engaged in rendering professional advice or services to the individual reader. The ideas, procedures, and suggestions contained in this book are not intended as a substitute for consulting with your physician. All matters regarding your health require medical supervision. Neither the author nor the publisher shall be liable or responsible for any loss, injury, or damage allegedly arising from any information or suggestion in this book.

ISBN 0-7394-5532-X

Printed in the United States of America

To my wife, Carrie,
whose beauty and joie de vivre
are my inspiration.
And to my children,
Daniel, Allison, Liza, and Jonathan,
who reaffirm my belief in the goodness of humanity.

ACKNOWLEDGMENTS

Thanks to my agent, Kris Dahl, who first believed in me and found this book a good home at Viking. The team at Viking was unmatched in its patience and professionalism throughout this project and I'd particularly like to thank my editor, Janet Goldstein, for her insights and encouragement. Thanks also to my cowriter, Cara Kagan, for her enormous contribution.

Caren Feingold also provided invaluable help with the nutritional information for this book, and Susanna Romano at AKS Salons for her tips on hairstyle and makeup.

Special thanks go to all my professors and mentors at New York University Department of Dermatology, Memorial Sloan-Kettering Institute, Wesleyan University, and Rockefeller University, who taught me the science of skin and to think analytically.

CONTENTS

Your Future Face

1

TAKING CHARGE OF YOUR SKIN

We are now in what I call the Golden Age of Skin Care. There have never before been so many products and procedures that can literally erase years off our faces. In fact, skin care, plastic surgery, and antiaging techniques are now frequently the topic of newspaper and magazine articles, TV news programs, and reality shows. Everywhere you look, it seems, there are new miracle ingredients and procedures designed to make you look younger than ever no matter what your age.

When it comes to turning back the clock, we are truly fortunate. No prior generation has had such an in-depth knowledge of the aging process as well as the chemistry and biological makeup of the skin. This knowledge has resulted in a dizzying number of amazing technological breakthroughs and a cornucopia of products and procedures that make it easier than ever to get a gorgeous and glowing complexion at any age.

But as media coverage and antiaging options have increased, it has become clear to me that many of my patients are really confused about what they should do for *their* skin. Often my patients come in with a magazine article or an ad for a product and ask me to explain it and to advise them on whether it is right for them. As modern technology increases and more ingredients and therapies are discovered, the more perplexed my patients become.

I decided that now more than ever it is crucial to clarify what is out there to help stop this confusion so that you can take charge of your skin and make fully educated decisions rather than relying on the recommendations of friends, the media, and product advertisements. I've written this book based on my sixteen years in private practice, the extensive research I've conducted in the antiaging area, and on the published studies of other prominent scientists and physicians. Its purpose is to help you choose the products and procedures that are right for *you* so you can beat father time at his own game. But more than presenting you with skin-care regimens and high-tech treatments, I want to help you tap into a powerful age-fighting weapon that is innate—your ability to predict how and when you are going to age and which areas are most vulnerable to its visible signs.

Sure, aging can seem like an overnight phenomenon. We go to bed one night with smooth, taut, glowing skin and wake up the next day somehow looking older. We may ask ourselves "How did this suddenly happen?" But no matter how much it seems like a sneak attack (and can it ever!), the aging process is actually systematic and predictable. And this is a beautiful thing. We have the power to look into the future and know what we can expect in terms of how we will look as we get older. This knowledge provides us with the most effective way to make our skin look better than ever today and to keep it looking that way well into tomorrow.

The key predictors are:

* Our genetics
* How our face looks when we are expressionless versus when it is expressing an emotion
* How we look when we are tired versus well rested
* How our skin has been affected by the sun. Sun-damaged skin often gets crinkles, which will ultimately turn into wrinkles.

Paying attention to these signals helps us determine how we will look as we get older and what areas of vulnerability we may have that might require a little extra TLC. And here is the best part: Once we know our specific aging patterns, we can take a targeted, results-oriented and, hence, more effective approach to getting beautiful, healthy, and more radiant-looking skin. And if you already have any early signs of time etched into your face, predicting their future impact will help you prevent these imperfections from becoming further entrenched and even erase many of them.

These days, selecting the skin-care regimens and treatments that will work best for us is more complicated than it was back when there were only *day* versus *night* creams to choose from. In this new era of walk-in, antiaging clinics, myriad skin-care products and treatments available in doctors' offices, spas, and stores, it is more important than ever to know what will help you get the right results for your face. Further complicating the matter is that it seems like a new wonder ingredient, product, or procedure is being introduced nearly every day. Some are actual miracle workers—proven by bona fide scientific research—to erase and prevent the signs of time. But some haven't yet proven themselves.

While this may not necessarily mean they won't some day, I strongly believe in going with the tried and true versus the not yet confirmed. This book will present and explain the scope of therapies currently on the market to help you weed out the ones that will be the most effective for you. By honing in on your specific needs, you can make the best possible decisions about the products and treatments that will give you the best results. The truth is, to get the benefits you are looking for, it is crucial that you use the products and procedures that address your specific patterns of aging at the appropriate phase of your skin's life cycle. Even if it is an ingredient or procedure with positive research behind it, not every anti-aging remedy is appropriate for *you* now, and some may never be.

The next chapter features my "Skin Life Cycle Quiz" that will determine the phase of your skin's development and your specific aging patterns. Then we will discuss the spectrum of treatments that will work best for you and help you develop your most effective regimen. In general, I have found that the vast majority of my patients get better results by starting out with milder but still efficacious products and treatments and gradually working their way up to stronger more aggressive ones if need be. Even if you are looking for a dramatic change, it's important to begin with the basics, such as wearing sunscreen and adhering to a solid daily regimen with proven active ingredients to help your skin get into the best possible condition it can be and then to keep it that way. Invasive procedures like face-lifts may turn back the clock, but they don't stop it from ticking. Time inevitably marches on. And while plastic surgery may tighten sagging skin, it won't improve your overall complexion. Meaning if your skin is blotchy, sun-damaged, and lined before the surgery, it will still be that way afterward.

Think of it this way. If we want to get in shape, going to the gym for the first time in years and hoisting the heaviest weights possible and running as fast as we can on the treadmill for five miles will most likely cause us to become injured—not become more fit. Our bodies respond better if we gradually increase the duration and intensity of our exercise routines. It is the cumulative effects of these consistent workouts that will help us to achieve our goals—not one extreme sweat session. Skin care operates in much the same way. Shocking the skin with an overly aggressive product or procedure can result in an injury that may outweigh any of its potentially positive effects. Over the years, I've treated hundreds of patients who've made enormous gains from nonaggressive products and procedures.

The Facts on Aging Skin

To understand better how to combat the signs of aging, it's a good idea to become familiar with the process itself. The rate at which our skin ages and how this aging will manifest itself are determined primarily by our genetics, the passage of time, and our lifestyles. All of these factors play a role in how we will look at any given moment and give us information to help predict how we will look in the future.

OUR FAMILY TREES

Our bodies have their own internal clocks that help determine how and when we will age. For some people, that clock ticks faster than others, and they look and/or feel older than their chronological years. For others, it ticks more slowly, and they look and/or feel younger. This clock is set by our ancestral DNA, which means there is a strong likelihood that our health and bodies, including our skin, will have the same strengths and weaknesses as those of our family members in much the same way as we inherit eye and hair color. Looking at the parent we most closely resemble and assessing how his or her skin aged can be a powerful predictor of how we will look in the future (see photo section, page 2). But lifestyle habits do play a role here. For example, if a parent smoked or worshiped the sun and you never did, your overall health and appearance will no doubt reap the benefits.

Knowing our inherent strengths and weaknesses lets us take the most targeted preventative and curative measures. For example, if sagging seems to be a family trait, there are lifestyle habits we can adopt, such as not losing a drastic amount of weight as we get older, to stave off the so-called inevitable. Our genetics also give us a good indication of which treatments and procedures will be the most effective for us. For example, if family members have been using an ingredient successfully without irritation, there is an excellent chance that it will have similar benefits for us.

AS TIME GOES BY

As we age our body's natural functions start to wind down, including the biochemical mechanisms that keep skin looking its best. Our skin has built-in natural defenses to protect it from damage, be it from a bad sunburn, drinking too much alcohol, not sleeping enough, and a host of other things. Skin also has amazing regenerative abilities that help it repair any damage it may have incurred. But our skin also has natural enzymes that break it down. As we age, our skin's defensive and healing powers no longer outpace its natural degradation process. The net result is that our skin loses its ability to fend off and recover from internal and external stressors.

Here's another fitness analogy. A young jogger can go out one day and pound the pavement. Her knees might be a bit sore afterward, but the next day she can get up and jog again without any major problems. An older jogger, whose knees have taken this type of stress for years, has less natural protection against this type of trauma and less than optimum regenerative abilities to help repair the damage her joints may have sustained during her afternoon run. She will most likely not be able to handle that kind of beating two days in a row without having aching knees. Our skin is no different. As we age, routine stresses, like the sun or lack of sleep, become more traumatic to our skin because we have fewer natural defenses to come to its aid. But here's where modern science steps in, bringing with it a host of protective and reparative products that can take over where our own natural functions have left off.

WEAR AND TEAR

When we buy a pair of new shoes, the leather is smooth, even in color, and blemish-free. But as we wear them, they start to develop creases. In the beginning, these creases are only visible when we are walking. But the more we walk in the shoes, the deeper the creases get until they are visible all the time. Our skin is kind of like that. The more we use it, the less "new" it appears. And we use our skin a lot. Our many years of making repetitive facial movements, for example, are a key cause of lines. If, let's say, we have a tendency to furrow our brows, our faces may "freeze that way," as our mothers might have said. Well, not exactly but close. What happens is that by constantly creasing our foreheads, we can tax the skin to the extent that its ability to bounce back becomes compromised. Gradually a wrinkle will form as a result, even when we are not furrowing (see photo section, page 3). But again, these creases don't have to be permanent. There are proven ways to relax them back either to their former smooth state or very close to it. Plus, there are many lifestyle habits we can adopt that will prevent further wear and tear and even reverse some of the signs of it. The sun, wind, not sleeping enough, eating an unhealthy diet, and many other habits do show up on our faces. By making certain changes in our daily routines, we not only can improve our overall health but also the condition of our skin.

Genetics also comes into play here, though. Some people are more predisposed than others to particular stresses. Think of that annoying friend who lives on cheeseburgers and fries yet remains superthin and doesn't develop high blood pressure. Once we factor in genetics with our skin's natural aging process and our lifestyle habits, we can develop a precise and targeted strategy that will put us on the path (and keep us there) to amazing-looking skin.

Amazing-looking skin, however, can be a completely subjective term. How we feel about the way we look plays a significant role when we are trying to determine an appropriate course of action. In my experience, a person who is happy with their appearance is pleased with making slow and steady improvements, even if others might say she needs a more speedy and radical approach. On the other hand, a person who is very critical of their appearance is often tempted to take more extreme measures in the hopes of making a dramatic difference, whether or not the condition of their skin calls for it.

But no matter how you feel about your skin, it is important to remember that permanent procedures such as a face-lift aren't reversible. And other invasive measures, such as laser resurfacing, which can be appropriate for some people, can leave lasting scars and skin discolorations.

Your first step to beautiful, younger-looking skin is to take all of these elements into account: your genetics, lifestyle, inherited patterns of aging, your skin's present condition, and the way you feel about your appearance so that you can make educated decisions about which products and therapies will work for you. "Creating Your Personal Profile" will help us determine your skin's level (phase of its life cycle) by factoring in all of the above. Your score will help you map out your personalized plan of products and perhaps procedures that will best work for you to give you the results that you want. Every level, however, does need to start out with the basic preventative measures and healthy skin-care habits outlined in chapter 3, "Level One: Essential Care and Prevention." Each successive chapter level will provide progressively more intensive measures that will yield more dramatic results. The important thing to remember, however, is that you don't *have* to get more aggressive and invasive if you are satisfied with the results you are getting and/or are just plain uncomfortable with the idea of elective cosmetic surgery or a procedure that requires substantial recovery time. It is *your* face, after all.

The last two chapters will focus on the lifestyle and nutritional habits that will make all the difference in the world to the way you look and feel—no matter what your level.

So with all this in mind, let's get started and give you the knowledge and the tools that will give you your best skin ever.

2

CREATING YOUR PERSONAL PROFILE

To help you develop your most effective regimen possible, I'm going to ask you to sharpen your diagnostic tools, most of which you already have. You'll start by determining the phase of your skin's development with "The Skin Life Cycle Quiz" and then you'll zero in on your specific areas of vulnerability by assessing the way you look now and by using the built-in age predictors specific to your face: your genetics; how your face looks when you are expressionless versus when you are expressing an emotion; how you look when you are tired versus well rested; how you've been affected by the sun so far—the crinkle-before-the-wrinkle test (see photo section, page 2); and your subjective feelings about your skin.

Then you will be armed and ready to take the most effective actions to treat your skin's exact conditions. *You,* not the label on a product, a facialist, friend, or the media, will design the regimen that will give you younger, healthier, and more beautiful skin.

The Skin Life Cycle Quiz

I developed a quiz so my patients and I are better able to zero in on which specific aspects of their appearance they would like to change and to what extent, what their inherited patterns of aging are, and how they really feel about the way that they look. These questions take into account four of the key components that help forecast how and when our skin will age.

How *you* score on this quiz will help you to determine the overall condition of your skin, or your *level*. Once we've figured that out, we will focus on the quiz's specific questions that will let us diagnose the areas or conditions that you might want to pay extra attention to. We will then customize the regimen of products, possible procedures, and lifestyle changes that will give you the best results in the most efficient and least invasive way.

The important thing to remember is that there is no such thing as being too young to start taking preventative measures or, conversely, having skin that is too far gone to make a difference. No matter what condition your skin is in, adopting solid, basic skin-care habits, a healthy diet and lifestyle, protecting yourself from the sun, and using the proven antiaging ingredients geared to your needs will make all the difference in the world—not only today but also for tomorrow. And if you decide you'd like to do more than the basics, knowing your level and specific areas of vulnerability will help you to sort through the hundreds of products and procedures on the market to determine the antiaging strategy that's best for *you*. With that in mind, rest easy in the knowledge that in this quiz, there is no such thing as a wrong answer. It is crucial that you respond to the questions as accurately and as honestly as possible, so you can find a safe and effective skin-care plan that is right for you.

Choose the single best answer for each of the following questions. And if you are currently receiving any treatments for correction of facial wrinkles (such as Botox or fillers), then answer the questions considering how your face would look *without* these treatments.

1. **How often do you think about the way your face looks?**
   A. Once a day
   B. Three times a day
   C. It's almost always on my mind

2. **Your past experience with the sun is:**
   A. You never burned
   B. You burned as a child and/or tanned as a teen
   C. You have burned in the past and already have had a skin cancer or precancer

3. **If you did not wear sunscreen and sat out in the sun, you would:**
   A. Tan immediately
   B. Turn red, then tan
   C. Most likely burn

4. **Now that you're an adult, when you're outdoors you:**
   A. Always wear at least an SPF 15
   B. Wear an SPF 15 but switch to a lower SPF once you're tan
   C. Use an SPF 8 or less

5. **When the family member you most closely resemble was your age, he or she looked:**
    A. Much worse than you do now
    B. Worse than you do now
    C. Better or the same as you do now

6. **(If you are female, answer this question in terms of your mother; if you are male, in terms of your father.) How did your mother or father's skin age?**
    A. Fabulously
    B. Acceptably
    C. Not well at all

7. **Your overall feeling about your skin is:**
    A. You are happy with the way that it is
    B. You are generally happy but there are one or two things that are starting to bother you
    C. There are a number of things that you'd like to change, and you're looking for fairly dramatic results

8. **You can honestly say that when it comes to leading a healthy lifestyle you:**
    A. Regularly eat right, get enough sleep, and exercise
    B. Regularly do two of the above
    C. Regularly do one or none of the above

9. **When you're tired your face:**
    A. Looks the same as when you've had a good night's sleep
    B. Has under-eye circles
    C. Has under eye-circles and bags

10. **How much do you smoke now or did you smoke in the past?**
    A. You do not smoke and never have

B. You smoke (d) one to four cigarettes daily

C. You smoke (d) five or more cigarettes every day

11. How much alcohol do you drink?

A. Scarcely any

B. Enough so that it affects your sleep once or twice a week

C. To intoxication once a week or more

12. Your forehead shows:

A. Two lines across it when you raise your eyebrows

B. More than two lines across it when you raise your eyebrows

C. Lines across it even when you don't raise your eyebrows

13. You think your forehead:

A. Looks fine but you want to prevent it from aging

B. Is okay for now but will probably start to show the signs of wear and tear in one to three years

C. Needs work to make you happy with it

14. The skin around your eyes (crow's-feet area) shows:

A. One to two lines when you smile

B. More than two lines when you smile

C. Lines even when you're not smiling

15. You think the skin around your eyes:

A. Looks fine but you want to prevent it from aging

B. Is okay for now but will probably start to show signs of wear and tear in one to three years

C. Could stand some noticeable improvement

16. Which of the following statements is most true about your eyelids?

    A.   Nothing bothers you about either the upper or lower eyelids

    B.   You are bothered either by wrinkles on the lower lid or laxity of the upper eyelid

    C.   You are bothered by both wrinkles on the lower eyelid and laxity on the upper eyelid

17. You think your eyelid skin:

    A.   Looks fine but you want to prevent it from aging

    B.   Is okay for now but will probably start to show some signs of wear and tear in one to three years

    C.   Could stand some noticeable improvement

18. Aging skin around the mouth changes in three ways: The creases deepen, the upper lip forms wrinkles, and the lips lose their plumpness. Which is true for you?

    A.   None of the above

    B.   One of the above

    C.   Two or three of the above

19. You think the skin around your mouth:

    A.   Looks fine but you want to prevent it from aging

    B.   Is okay for now but will probably start to show some signs of wear and tear in one to three years

    C.   Could stand some noticeable improvement

20. You neck skin is:

    A.   Firm and does not bother you

    B.   Shows some laxity

    C.   Sags too much

21. You think your neck:

A. Looks fine but you want to prevent it from aging

B. Is okay for now but will probably start to show some signs of wear and tear in one to three years

C. Could stand some noticeable improvement

22. The skin on the back of your hands:

A. Is firm and does not bother you

B. Does not bounce back quickly after you pinch and release it

C. Sags too much

23. You think your hands:

A. Look fine but you want to prevent them from aging

B. Are okay for now but will probably start to show some signs of wear and tear in one to three years

C. Could stand some noticeable improvement

Calculating your final score

Follow the directions below, especially those in **bold.**

Count the number of times you selected answer A. Enter that number in the box below.	Count the number of times you selected answer B. **Multiply it by 2.** Enter that number in the box below.	Count the number of times you selected answer C. **Multiply it by 3.** Enter that number in the box below.
☐	☐	☐

Add the numbers in the 3 boxes above: ⬭

If you are 33 years old or older enter 5 here: ⬭

Add the circled numbers together for your final score: ⬭

FINAL SCORE

(A score of 23–34)   Level One: Essential Care and Prevention

I call this phase in your skin's life cycle Invisible Aging because while your skin may appear youthful and beautiful on the surface, deep down below it's already starting to age. "Level One: Essential Care and Prevention" will help you plan out a customized plan of sound daily skin care and lifestyle habits, plus identify the products that will help keep you looking fabulous longer and prevent those invisible signs from surfacing. The "Level Two Active Repair and Protection" chapter will outline some slightly more aggressive preemptive and curative measures that you may want to take as your skin progresses to the next level. These treatments also may be relevant if you feel like you have one or two issues that seem to be "older" than the rest of your face or a strong genetic tendency toward something you'd rather not be faced with; e.g., deep lines in the crow's-feet area. At this phase, you shouldn't even think about doing any *major* corrective or preventative measures for at least the next one to three years or even more. Retake this quiz in six months to a year to chart your progress and to ensure that your regimen is effective.

(A score of 35–46)   Level Two: Active Repair and Protection

At this point, you are starting to see what I call Surface Signs— meaning some of the aging that was going on down below is now visible. But while your skin is starting to undergo some changes, you feel good about the way you look overall. It's important for you to maintain these positive feelings about yourself, no matter how much pressure the media and/or peers exert(s). Now is not the time to pull out any of the big guns and go for any major or permanent procedures, such as a deep acid peel, laser resurfacing, or plastic surgery. You'll begin with "Level One: Essential Care and Prevention" to map out your basic skin-care regimen to help prevent further damage and reverse some of what you've already incurred. The good news? These measures might be all that you need to get the skin you've always wanted. If you want to be somewhat more assertive in preventing and/or in correcting any issues that are bothering you, turn to chapter 4, "Level Two: Active Repair and Protection," which will explain the menu of slightly more aggressive proactive and corrective options available to you and help you to choose which one(s) will give you the best results. Chapter 5, "Level Three: Age-Erasing Options," will reveal some more intensive ways to handle the areas that seem to be aging faster than the rest of your face and/or some other tactics you may want to consider taking as you progress to the next level. Retake this quiz in six months to a year to chart your progress and to ensure that your regimen is effective.

(A score of 47–58)   Level Three: Age-Erasing Options

Your skin is now in a phase where you will notice what I call Deeper Damage. For this reason, you would like to make some changes—perhaps even some fairly dramatic ones. You may have an overall score of Level Three, but on further analysis your face may have one significantly worse area (your eyes, for example) while the rest of your face is Level Two. Many people are a combination of levels (see "Aging Patterns of Different Facial Areas" in the photo section). But the world is still your oyster and the opportunities abound for getting and maintaining healthier, younger-looking, and more glowing skin. I recommend starting with the basics and then gradually working your way up the ladder in terms of aggressiveness, if need be. Little changes can still make a huge difference. You'll begin with "Level One: Essential Care and Prevention" to learn your basic antiaging regimen and to find out the lifestyle changes you can make to put you on the path to a radiant complexion. "Level Two: Active Repair and Protection" will introduce the more intensive defensive and offensive measures that will make more noticeable and dramatic improvements when used in tandem with an effective daily skin-care regimen. Should you still want to turn up the heat, "Level Three: Age-Erasing Options" will explain all of the more aggressive antiaging procedures, help you weigh their promised benefits against their risks, and outline when and in what combination they might work best for your needs. "Level Four: Major Changes . . . Or Not" will evaluate some of the ways you can treat the areas that seem to be aging faster than the rest of your face, and how to plan accordingly. Retake this quiz in six months to a year to chart your progress and to ensure your regimen is effective.

(A score of 59 plus) Level Four: Major Changes . . . Or Not

At this level, your skin is at what I call the Advanced Aging stage. This might mean that there are many things about your appearance you'd like to change significantly. But now is not the time to panic and seek out the most extreme measures. "Level Four: Major Changes . . . Or Not" does give you a suggested timeline for using the more aggressive age-beaters, including cosmetic surgery, if you want more of a dramatic change. Again, while your overall score is Level Four some of your face may only be a Level Three or even Level Two! But good daily skin-care habits, proven antiaging ingredients, and diligent use of sunscreen are still important parts of your regimen, no matter which procedure or surgery you may choose to undergo. There is also a wide array of noninvasive in-office treatments that can also help you make noticeable and positive changes. Review the strategies in Levels One to Three to see which options will give you the best results within your comfort level.

Your Visible Signs of Aging— Do You Have Problem Areas?

Now that you've determined your level, let's zero in on your particular areas of vulnerability. If any of these problems are already visible *and* they bother you, place a check mark next to them. These are the issues to which you might want to consider giving a little extra TLC, in addition to following a good skin-care regimen and leading a healthy lifestyle. This way, we can fine-tune the precise plan of attack that will be the most effective for you. I will address treatment for these issues at each level moving from the least invasive therapies to the most dramatic ones.

THE VISIBLE SIGNS OF AGING

Wrinkles
Lines
General laxity
Sagging around the jaw and neck
Brow furrows
Eye wrinkles or crow's-feet
Bags under the eyes

Slack upper eyelids

Lines on the forehead and/or from the nose to the
    mouth

Pigmentation spots

Broken capillaries

Enlarged pores

Your Aging Patterns: What Problems Can You Predict and Minimize?

You can forecast the areas of concern that are not yet visible but may crop up later on in life. As you read through the factors below, make a note of the particular risks that seem to apply to you.

OUR GENETICS (PHOTO SECTION, PAGE 2)

Looking at the parent you most closely resemble literally can serve as a blueprint for the way we will most likely look when we are older. Is there a family trait? Are there any signs of aging, such as brow furrows, crow's-feet, or under-eye bags that nearly everyone seems to have? Looking beyond what we see in the mirror today and at the older face that's most like ours can forecast how we will look tomorrow. But don't forget that lifestyle habits can have a profound affect here, as well as speeding up or slowing down the aging process. One of my daughters, for example, has had frown lines in between her brows when she scowls or concentrates since practically the day she was born. They're inherited from her family. But knowing this is her area of vulnerability will help her to prevent them from becoming more entrenched. Practical advice I'll give my daughter is to diligently wear sunglasses to minimize her scowling in the sun. This will help prevent permanent creasese between her brows to which she is predisposed.

HOW YOU LOOK WHEN YOU ARE EXPRESSIONLESS VERSUS WHEN YOU ARE EXPRESSING AN EMOTION (PHOTO SECTION, PAGE 3)

In a sense, year after year of repetitive facial movements act like a stressor to the skin. There is a strong possibility that the lines or furrows that only appear when we squint, for example, may become permanent later on in life. These areas reveal our face's weakest links—the places that are selectively vulnerable because they experience and have experienced the most stress.

HOW YOU LOOK WHEN YOU'RE TIRED VERSUS WELL RESTED (PHOTO SECTION, PAGE 2)

Do you have dark circles? Puffy under eyes? Does your face seem more slack or pinched? How we look when we are tired today also can be a predictive mirror of what our faces may look like tomorrow even when we aren't tired. The reason? When we are younger and well rested our body is essentially running on a full tank of gas—meaning our reserves and regenerative abilities are at optimum levels. At the end of the day, as our tank becomes depleted, if we get a good night's sleep, we wake up on full. One or two sleepless nights don't necessarily affect our appearance because our reserves are strong enough to survive a few days without refueling.

As we mature, our skin's reserves are more easily depleted and so we temporarily look older when we don't get enough rest. The areas of our face that appear more aged as a result reflect our areas of vulnerability. They can reveal what we may look like once we have exhausted our reserves. When we are older, no matter how much sleep we get, we still have fewer reserves and regenerative abilities so we may end up looking tired all of the time, even when we aren't.

HOW YOUR SKIN HAS BEEN DAMAGED BY THE SUN—THE CRINKLE-BEFORE-THE-WRINKLE PRINCIPLE (PHOTO SECTION, PAGE 2)

Areas of skin that appear crinkly though not quite lined or wrinkled, either all the time or just after a pinch is released, generally indicate areas that have sustained more sun damage than the rest of the face or the body. The chest, eye area, and hands are especially vulnerable to crinkling. Over time, there is a strong possibility that these regions will morph into lines, or wrinkles, or start to sag.

Now go back to the list of "The Visible Signs of Aging," page 21, and place an X next to the issues that haven't yet appeared but seem likely to. Anything with an X or a check mark are your specific areas of vulnerability, which are addressed for each skin level throughout the book.

We will now start at the beginning. Whatever your age and current skin-care approach, I have found that it's invaluable to put together the right state-of-the-art regimen. It will help your skin live up to its full potential of health, radiance, and beauty, minimize and sometimes even eliminate the need for more involved treatments, and help your skin derive the maximum benefits from any products or procedures you decide to use.

3
Level One

ESSENTIAL CARE AND PREVENTION

For the most part, my Level One (a score of 23–34) patients are in skin heaven. Most of them have banished any of the blemishes they may have had in high school and/or college, though some are still prone to breakouts that only seem to occur mid-menstrual cycle. Their skin is taut, smooth, unlined, and fairly radiant. They are generally in their twenties to midthirties, and any concerns they have are fairly minor—a few sunspots here, perhaps a cluster of broken capillaries there. If you are in Level One, you probably haven't yet moved into the phase where the more serious signs of sun damage have appeared, though there may be crinkling with the tiniest hint of crow's-feet or the faintest forehead furrow.

My mantra for Level Ones is the tried but true: "an ounce of prevention . . ."—well, you know the rest. The thing about skin at this phase is that even if it appears unmarred on the surface, it can be undergoing changes deep down inside that will start to affect its appearance not too far down the road. Credible scientific research shows that as early as age twenty-five our skin's two structural proteins—collagen (which keeps it firm, taut, and resilient) and elastin (which gives skin its flexibility, enabling it to stretch out and then snap back into place)—decrease. Futhermore, cell turnover slows, antioxidant protection diminishes, and natural defenses and skin-healing abilities decline. Not to sound dramatic, but here is the reality: You may not be able to see lines or wrinkles or sagging, but they are there hiding below the surface; and they will, not long from now, start to become visible.

But enough doom and gloom. The good news is that we can, in fact, fight Mother Nature and even finesse our genetics in some ways. During the last decade an exciting number of ingredients and treatments have proven themselves to be effective in slowing down our skin's natural aging process, and even reversing some of its signs. Your skin can look fabulous longer than we've ever thought possible, and you can face the coming years ahead far more beautifully than anyone ever imagined.

The Basics

Your plan of attack is to protect your skin from further damage, to prolong its present youthful state, and to prevent those signs of aging from surfacing for as long as possible. And you can do all of the above by incorporating just a few essential practices and active ingredients—with documented evidence behind them—into your everyday life. These habits will not only significantly improve your skin's health and appearance today but also guarantee that it will look firm and radiant in the future.

When Cost Counts

When it comes to skin care, money *may* buy more effective higher tech or medical-grade ingredients that justify the price tag, but not always. Some expensive sunscreens, for example, contain the same basic ingredients as the cheaper ones. But in general, the more expensive products are more esthetically pleasing to use in terms of their texture, scent, and packaging.

1. ASSESS YOUR SKIN TYPE

I frequently see Level One and even Level Two patients who continue to use the same harsh cleansers and drying astringents they relied on when they were oily and acne-prone teenagers. While these products won't age skin, they can compromise its health and appearance. You may not feel or see it, but at this phase in your skin's life cycle, your oil glands are starting to shrink so they start to produce less sebum. This can make antiacne and mattifying products that were once effective cause redness, flaking, and irritation. Logically, you might try to alleviate this discomfort by switching to a heavier moisturizer or applying one more frequently but, unfortunately, this seemingly appropriate remedy only exacerbates the problem. Level One skin is particularly prone to breakouts, as well as clogged and/or permanently enlarged pores, that can occur from moisturizing overkill.

Dried-out skin also may try to rebound and produce even more oil to lubricate itself. This can lead to more blemishes, which may prompt you to use even stronger drying agents in an attempt to clear them up. Alcohol-based products, especially, are notorious for causing this boomerang effect. Using them may also lead to the hyperirritation that can cause the formation of broken capillaries and exacerbate rosacea and eczema.

If the use of antiacne products is drying out your skin, or if your skin is simply becoming drier on its own, first try using a milder cleanser (e.g., one that is labeled for NORMAL/COMBINATION or SENSITIVE skin instead of one for OILY or BLEMISH-PRONE, skin) before you switch to a more emollient moisturizer or start to use a moisturizer more frequently. Also, if you use a toner, try switching from an alcohol-based product to one that contains witch hazel. The extract from this plant has a proven astringent, toning, and anti-inflammatory effects. It also dissolves excess sebum without stripping skin. I purposely formulated M.D. Skincare's cleanser with witch hazel as research shows it has all of these benefits without the potential side effects of alcohol.

If you've taken these measures and your skin is still dry and tight, the best way to soothe it without causing additional breakouts is to use a moisturizer that is labeled OIL FREE. These lotions increase the water content of skin without adding extra oil, so they won't aggravate or cause acne. Start by applying the moisturizer once a day and then trade up to twice daily if you need it. Believe it or not, products that are labeled with terms like NON-COMEDOGENIC, HYPOALLERGENIC, FOR ACNE-PRONE SKIN, and WON'T CLOG PORES that suggest they do not cause breakouts can contain oil, which can clog pores and cause blemishes.

If your skin is dry in certain areas, such as the cheeks, but continues to be oily in others, such as your forehead, nose, and chin (also known as the T-zone), you can remedy the situation by applying a basic moisturizer on just the spots that are dry or by using a "self-adjusting" formula on your whole face. This type of product contains special moisturizing ingredients that only cling to dry areas.

2. REV UP CELL RENEWAL: DAILY EXFOLIATION

A healthy rate of skin cell renewal, also known as cell turnover, is one of the key components of radiant and even-toned skin. When we are teenagers, dead skin cells slough off when they are supposed to, so we don't typically develop any flaky, dead-skin buildup that can dull our complexions. Throughout our twenties and thirties, however, surface cell turnover starts to slow down from about every twenty-eight days in our teens to roughly thirty-five days at age thirty-five. While a seven-day lag may not seem like much, it can take its toll on skin. An accumulation of dead cells makes skin thicker, rougher, and prevents it from appearing radiant. But giving sluggish cell turnover a booster shot is a breeze; it merely requires some daily exfoliation. To avoid irritation, I recommend starting with the mildest method and then gradually working up to stronger ones only if necessary.

Cleansing with a fresh washcloth with a very light pressure and circular motions might be all you need to gently remove most dead-skin cells. (**PLEASE NOTE** that using the same washcloth more than one time may lead to breakouts and irritation because cloths can harbor bacteria and mold.) The next step up would be to use a witch hazel–based toner once a day, which will work a little harder than the cloth to exfoliate.

If your skin still appears dull, you can add a little more oomph in your exfoliation regime by using a moisturizer, gel, or serum with beta hydroxy (salicylic acid) and/or alpha hydroxy acids. Both types of acids work by weakening the links between cells in the outer layers of dry skin to allow the normal shedding process to occur at a more optimum rate. They may also play a role in building skin-firming collagen and elastin, especially when incorporated into a two-step chemical peel. Alpha hydroxy acids include: lactic (from dairy products), glycolic (from sugar), malic (from apples), and citric (from citrus fruits.) Salicylic acid is synthetic

but close to the molecular structure of an acid that occurs naturally in skin, making it generally nonirritating. It is the only beta
hydroxy acid currently used in skin-care products. In my research
I have found that lotions and creams with several different kinds
of acids are the most effective and least irritating because when
many different acids are combined, each one can be used in a
lower (i.e., milder) concentration.

As far as manual exfoliants, such as scrubs with granules or
sloughing sponges, are concerned, I find that many people over-
use them and/or scrub too vigorously. But when used carefully
and as directed, they can be effective. If you like using a scrub,
look for one that contains perfectly round smooth polyethylene
beads, which are gentler than seeds, nuts, husks, or pits.

3. GO ON THE DEFENSIVE:
PREVENT SUN DAMAGE

It's no secret that the sun is our skin's worst enemy when it comes
to causing signs of premature aging. Its ultraviolet rays are the
most active culprits in triggering free radicals. These highly destructive, corrosive, and electrically charged molecules are a leading cause of everything from heart disease to arthritis. In the case
of skin, free radicals are like little darts that poke holes in our collagen and elastin. Eventually, free radicals corrode these stuctural
proteins—literally eating away their integrity. Think of how rusty
metal starts to crumble after a certain point.

Getting in the habit of wearing sunscreen with an SPF 15 or
higher every day, even when you are not planning to spend a lot
of time outdoors, is a surefire way to help prevent free radicals from
forming and can prevent the damage they cause. Research shows
that a substantial amount of premature aging comes from incidental sun exposure when we're unaware of it—such as when

we're out shopping or even grabbing lunch. Wearing sunscreen every day will help to prevent the signs of premature aging.

Maeve,* twenty-three, had very fair skin with sunspots and a chronically pink nose—the result of sun damage. Maeve came to me because she was unhappy that she had so many freckles, but I was more concerned by her nose. Skin that is chronically pink typically has undergone damage to its DNA and may be prone to skin cancer. While Maeve did wear SPF 15, she wore it sporadically, and she wasn't applying enough of it when she did. We increased her daily sunscreen to SPF 30 and improved her application habits—making sure she used enough and covered sufficient ground with it. Now both of us are happy. Because she isn't continually causing more damage, her freckles are much fainter and her nose far less pink. The lesson here is that when you stop making something worse, the skin can heal itself and look better naturally.

Sunscreen 101

Even the most religious sunscreen users can damage their skin because of some simple oversights. Here are a few new golden rules for practicing safe sun:

1. Wear It Every Day, Even in Winter

Since sun damage can occur during even short periods of sun exposure, it's a great idea to make applying it every morning second nature, like brushing your teeth or combing your hair. And while the sun may feel its strongest in July and August, it is possible to sustain sun damage all year-round, even on cloudy days. And if there is snow on the ground, it can increase the chance of sun dam-

*The name has been changed.

age because it reflects the sunlight on the ground back up to your face, in much the same way as the sand on the beach. The sun's ultraviolet rays also can, to some degree, penetrate glass, so unless the windows are specifically treated with UV protection, you can incur sun damage sitting in front of the window of your sun-filled living room, in your office, driving your car, and on an airplane.

2. Go Broad and Go Higher

The most beneficial sunscreens are broad spectrum. This means they offer protection against UVA and UVB rays, which are both detrimental to skin. There has been much debate as to whether SPFs higher than 15 "really do anything," but I have recently changed my recommendation from an SPF 15 to an SPF 30 for baseline protection when you are going to be outdoors for extended periods of time. An SPF 15 blocks out 92 percent of the sun's rays. An SPF 30 blocks out 96 percent, and an SPF 45 or higher blocks out 97 percent. But it is doubtful that SPF 45 is really more effective than SPF 30. SPF 30, however, offers significantly more protection than SPF 15. While a 4 percent increase in protection may not seem like a lot, to your body it is, and the difference between an SPF 15 and SPF 30 is huge. The human body is so highly fine-tuned that even the slightest variation can help or harm it. Think of it this way: If a 140-pound woman loses 4 percent of her body weight, she will lose almost 6 pounds. In all likelihood the absence of those 6 extra pounds will make a difference in the way her clothes fit and probably in how she feels.

I recommend daily use of the higher SPFs and frequent reapplication if avoiding the sun isn't possible—though it is advisable. It is doubly important for people getting laser treatments and peels, and/or using bleaching products, Retin-A or Renova, or Accutane. All of these therapies make your skin more susceptible to sun damage, as do other medications, including certain antibiotics and birth-control pills. Always ask your physician about this whenever you are prescribed a new medication.

3. Pick Your Perfect Formulation

Many of my patients don't use sun protection because it has made them break out in the past. If you have oily and/or blemish-prone skin, go with an oil-free version to prevent your sunblock from exacerbating your condition. In addition, all skin types are better served by using a formulation geared specifically to the face rather than the one you use on your body; those formulated for the face are less greasy and less irritating.

4. Love It

Sunscreen only helps if you put it on. So find one with a texture, finish, and scent that you really like. This way, you'll have absolutely no problem adding it to your daily regimen and reapplying it as needed.

5. Time It Right

It's important to apply chemical sunscreens (for example, ones which contain octyl methoxycinamate, octocylene, or avobenzene) at least 30 minutes prior to sun exposure so these ingredients can react with skin. These types of products absorb the sun's energy, diverting it away from us. Physical sunblocks, such as titanium dioxide or zinc oxide, work immediately; they literally form a protective shield over our skin.

6. Be Generous

A classic error in sunscreen application (for even the most die-hard user) is not using enough. To be truly protected, we need to use *a lot* of sunscreen—about two to four ounces to cover your face and body, depending on your size. We also need to reapply it every three to four hours and immediately after swimming or heavily perspiring (even if you are using a waterproof variety). Reapplication is also key to protecting skin from sun damage.

7. Don't Forget Often Overlooked Places

To fully shield your forehead, it is important to work sunscreen at least 1/2 inch into the hairline rather than applying it across your forehead in the side-to-side motion most people use. Two other often neglected areas are the ears and the scalp. Both regions are endowed with very little protective pigment and can easily become burned and develop skin cancer. Protecting your lips is equally important.

8. Resist the Temptation to "Get as Tan as You Used To"

Many of my patients often say somewhat wistfully to me that they just can't achieve that perfect shade of golden brown that they used to during their childhood and teens. There is nothing wrong with their vacation or suntanning regimen. Failing to get tan actually means your skin has "burned out" its own natural sun protection, melanin. Repeated sun exposure and burning can damage the skin's melanocytes, the cells that produce melanin or pigment, so the body may no longer be able to produce enough melanin to let you tan or tan as deeply as you used to. Some people also develop white spots on certain areas, which means that the melanocytes there have literally died because of an overdose of sun exposure. If you've experienced either or both of these conditions, it means your body requires extra sun protection—not additional hours of sunbathing.

9. Rethink Pink

A burn, unfortunately, isn't the only sign of damage. Turning pink isn't so great for you either. Pinkness is actually the sign of a little burn. Skin that is chronically pinkened by the sun may also be undergoing a mutation to its DNA, which is associated with all types of skin cancers. Areas that stay pink permanently mean that they have lost many of their melanocytes. These regions require either more frequent sunscreen application or a higher SPF than the one you are using everywhere else. The nose is more vulnerable to becoming permanently pink than other parts of the face because it is the most exposed to the ultraviolet rays. For this reason, it is the most common area for skin cancers. The chest is another especially susceptible area. If any part of your face or body turns the slightest bit pink, it's best to apply a higher SPF there, even if it means using two different sunscreens.

10. Beat the Heat

During the hottest hours of the day—from roughly 10 A.M. to 3:00 P.M.—it's a good idea to seek out some shade. The reason? The sun's heat, not just its ultraviolet rays, decomposes the skin's vital proteins. Think of a steak left in the broiler. Even when you turn off the flame the meat continues to cook and shrivel up. It may have started out as rare but now, all of a sudden, it's well done.

4. FIGHT FREE RADICALS:
LOADING UP ON ANTIOXIDANTS

As crucial as wearing sunscreen on a daily basis is to the health and appearance of our skin, studies have shown that many products may not be 100 percent effective in safeguarding us from sun damage. Some ultraviolet rays can still penetrate skin and spark the formation of dartlike free radicals.

Our skin, ingenious organ that it is, contains enzymes and natural antioxidants that help neutralize and protect it against free radicals. Antioxidants are substances that prevent free radicals from causing oxidative damage, which is what leads to the wearing away of collagen and elastin. If free radicals are like little darts poking holes in our collagen and elastin, then antioxidants are the decoy targets that prevent them from hitting their mark.

As we age, our bodies no longer create these antioxidants and enzymes in the quantities we need to fend off these sneak free-radical attacks. Their production starts to slow down even as early as our twenties. But modern science has put us at a tremendous advantage by discovering naturally occurring ingredients that when ingested and/or applied topically help disarm free radicals the moment they form, and even prevent them from forming in the first place.

So far, antioxidant vitamins C and E have proven to be among the best free-radical scavengers. There is increasing medical evidence that they reduce the incidence of a number of serious diseases, plus diminish and even reverse the signs of aging. There have also been studies with extremely positive findings about lycopene, which is found in tomatoes, watermelon, and red grapes; green tea extract; white tea extract; beta-carotene, a pro-vitamin A, found in carrots and dark leafy greens; bioflavanoids found in blueberries and raspberries; anthocyanins, also found in red grapes; and P. emblica, extracts from the fruit, bark, and/or leaves from the Phyllanthus emblica tree.

Incorporating these nutrients into your diet and as ingredients in your skin regimen can yield many health and beauty benefits. M.D. Skincare's Antioxidant Face-Firming Complex contains a cocktail of all these antioxidants, which I believe is more effective than formulas containing only one or two antioxidants. (See chapter 8 for more information on these nutrients.)

As with exfoliating acids, I recommend using products that incorporate as many different kinds of antioxidants as possible. New research has indicated that there are at least two different kinds of free radicals—those triggered by the body (metabolic) and those sparked by the sun and other environmental assailants. Furthermore, some antioxidants work better in different portions of the skin because some are lipid soluble while others are water soluble. So far, studies have shown that lycopene is excellent at fending off environmental free radicals. Vitamin E is strong in disabling the metabolic variety. Vitamin C seems to combat both. Meanwhile, promising studies are now showing that green and white tea extracts not only can fight both types of free radicals but that they also repair DNA. Damaged DNA increases aging, reduces our defenses against free radicals, diminishes our cells' regenerative ability, and can even result in skin cancer.

5. BOOST COLLAGEN AND ELASTIN PRODUCTION: THE A AND C VITAMINS CONNECTION

When our skin processes are functioning optimally, they are in a state of what is called *dynamic equilibrium*—meaning our capability to regenerate collagen and elastin keeps pace with their natural degeneration. As time goes by, we have less and less of an ability to maintain dynamic equilibrium, so these proteins begin to degenerate faster than our body can repair them. In addition, not to be a harbinger of bad news, but credible scientific research shows that at age thirty, collagen and elastin production starts to decline in quantity and quality. There are many proven ingredients with exciting research behind them, however, that can help us forestall and even reverse this process.

Vitamin C, so far, has proven to be one of the strongest catalysts of collagen growth especially when it's applied topically. Using products that incorporate this nutrient, as well as eating foods that contain it, can significantly improve that quality and quantity of the collagen we produce, which will make skin firmer, more radiant, and healthier-looking today, and help keep it looking that way tomorrow. And although taking oral vitamin C is important and healthy (see chapter 8), applying it topically is the most potent way to get its antiaging benefit for your skin. If you do the math, one would need to eat more than one hundred 250mg vitamin C pills (which is highly toxic!) to get the same amount of vitamin C to your skin provided by simply applying a 5 percent vitamin C cream.

Retinoids, derivatives of vitamin A, have also proven to be important parts of the antiaging arsenal. Studies have shown that they stimulate the production of new skin cells and inhibit the body's natural enzymes that break down collagen. At Level One, using retinol, the nonprescription strength variety, should do the trick. Prescription-strength tretinoin, which is the key ingredient in Retin-A and Renova, is indeed a more potent wrinkle fighter, but it can also be irritating and increase your skin's sensitivity to the sun. Incorporating both vitamin C and retinol into a daily skin-care regimen will help to tackle erosion of both collagen and elastin safely and effectively.

There are other antioxidants and collagen builders that have some positive data behind them, but the findings are less clear. For example, copper peptides, proteins merged with copper and iron that occur naturally in skin seem to play a role in collagen and elastin formation. Some studies have shown that when applied topically, copper peptides can significantly reduce the signs of sun damage and improve faint to moderate lines and wrinkles. Coenzyme Q-10 (a.k.a. ubiquinone) might also be another collagen builder. This compound is made by our bodies and used by our cells to produce the energy they need to grow and be healthy. Also an antioxidant with actions very similar to those of vitamin E, coenzyme Q-10 has been found in some studies to be an excellent defender against free radicals and when used regularly, over time, it may help ease lines and wrinkles by building collagen. In addition, some studies have suggested that kinetin, a naturally occurring growth hormone found in plants and animals, has antioxidant properties and may play a role in stimulating collagen synthesis. Peptides are among the newest collagen-boosting ingredients used in products such as Strivectin, which incorporates pentatpepide–3. All of these ingredients may or may not prove to be excellent age beaters, and more research is needed to establish their benefits. Stay tuned.

6. PAMPER YOUR UNDER-EYE AREA: STAVING OFF THE VERY FIRST SIGNS OF AGING

Most of my Level One patients kick off their antiaging regimen by starting to use a moisturizing under-eye cream or gel. Typically, that is the first part of the face to look a little worse for wear. This is because the skin there is especially thin and so more prone to the lines caused by wear and tear and sun damage.

While a moisturizing eye cream will keep the area looking plump and dewy, using one that also contains antioxidants, sunscreen, vitamin C, and retinol is an even better way to go. Wearing a product with sunscreen and antioxidants during the day will help to prevent sun damage and free-radical formation. Using a cream or gel with vitamin C and retinol at night will help to jump-start collagen content. I recommend using products specifically created for the under-eye region, rather than ones for the face, because they have been formulated to be extra gentle on this especially sensitive area.

Reading and working in a well-lit room, wearing sunglasses outside, and wearing the right corrective lenses for any vision problems will all help to minimize the wear and tear we unwittingly cause to the skin under and around our eyes every time we squint. And while this may seem nitpicky, resisting the urge to rub itchy eyes will also help to reduce the amount of stress this area is subjected to.

To Moisturize or Not to Moisturize?

While it has been marketed as *the* cornerstone of an antiaging skin-care regimen for at least a century, moisturizers actually won't turn back the clock; they are merely an effective way to alleviate dry skin. So if you have Level One skin and it isn't dry, you don't need a moisturizer. (**PLEASE NOTE:** If your skin is Level Two or higher, turn to chapter 4 for *your* moisturizing specifics.) Instead, you can find active antiaging ingredients, such as vitamin C and alpha hydroxy acids, in pads, gels, and serums that won't add unnecessary oil to skin. But if even after switching to a milder cleanser your skin is still dry and flaky, it's a sign that it needs additional moisture.

To help prevent the clogged pores and blemishes to which Level One skin is prone, I recommend starting out by using a moisturizer in the form of a lotion, which is the lightest weight and so the least likely to cause breakouts. If your skin still needs more moisture, move up to a cream version, which has more oil in it. The next step would be to switch to formulations geared to "extra dry," followed by those for "severely dry" skin if necessary.

You might find it necessary to switch moisturizers or adjust their frequency from time to time, such as with the change of seasons, or depending on what other products you are using.

First to Last:
The Right Order for Your Basics

One of the keys to maximizing the benefits of any product in your daily skin-care regimen is to apply products with a thinner consistency before the thicker more creamy ones, *no matter what their active ingredients are.* Products with heavy consistencies can block lighter-weight ones from penetrating the skin and doing their job. Here is a sample application order:

1. Liquids, such as antiacne or light peel pads for exfoliating and collagen building, or any kind of toner.

2. Serums or gels, which are more viscous than a liquid but less so than a lotion and can do everything from moisturize to deliver vitamin C or offer sun protection.

3. Lotions, which are milky, slightly thicker liquids, and can include moisturizers, moisturizers with sunscreens, and moisturizers with antioxidants or exfoliating acids.

4. Creams, which can do all of the above but are thicker, richer substances that won't spill out of a jar if it's turned over.

5. Ointments, generally petrolatum-based solids that come in a tube and squeeze out very slowly, such as Vaseline.

The exception to this rule of thumb is that any form of sun protection, be it in a moisturizer or not, must be applied before any other product (except a liquid). Its defensive ingredients need to cling directly to skin in order to be most effective.

Apply products to cool, dry skin to ensure their effectiveness as well as decrease the chances of irritation. Water, even microscopic droplets, also can prevent active ingredients from penetrating. After toweling dry, it's a good idea to wait an extra minute or so to make sure that any remaining water has totally evaporated. But here is another tricky exception: If you are just putting on a moisturizer without any other active ingredient, it's best to apply it immediately after toweling off to seal in additional moisture.

It's also wise to let any redness fade after showering or cleansing before using any treatment product. When skin is red, all of its vital functions are struggling to help it return to a calmer state, so any active ingredient might be more than it can handle at that given moment. When skin is in this recover mode, products that it otherwise might have been able to tolerate can prolong the redness and make it appear irritated.

Food for Thought

Facials and Masks: Are They Antiaging?

Facials: Many of my Level One patients start to get facials regularly at this time in their lives thinking that they are a way to preserve a youthful complexion. But there is no data supporting the antiaging claims often made for facials. Facials for the most part pamper, moisturize, deep cleanse, make skin more beautiful, and give the face a temporarily more refreshed and rejuvenated appearance. Some spas, however, recently have incorporated bona fide antiaging treatments into their menus, including multiacid peels and facials incorporating vitamin C. These treatments can help rev up our skin's collagen-boosting machinery. Peels are especially effective when coupled with facials, which by design exfoliate dead skin cells so any active ingredient can penetrate the skin better.

Masks: Similar to facials, masks are not fountains of youth, but they can provide an intensive way to help remedy a host of skin problems, such as dullness through exfoliation; dryness through concentrated moisturization; blemishes through deep cleansing and drying up excess oil; eye puffiness through anti-inflammatory ingredients, or large pores through sloughing out the debris that stretches them out in the first place. When used as directed they complement but do not replace a solid antiaging daily regimen.

Monitoring Your Results

Unfortunately, there is no way to know in advance how well a product will work. Companies aren't required to list the percentages or strengths of main active ingredients on labels of nonprescription products, unless they are classified as a drug. And often a product's efficacy is based on a combination of ingredients rather than each one's concentration. A product or regimen may not make a huge visible difference now to Level One skin because it is used more to prevent *future* damage and optimize the skin's vital functions rather than to turn back the clock. But good skin care today makes all the difference in how we will look tomorrow.

Still, taking these largely preventative measures should improve the overall condition and appearance of your skin. It should become smoother, more radiant, and evenly toned. Here is a key rule of thumb: If you don't notice some kind of positive change after four to six weeks of using a product, try something else. On the other hand, stop using a product immediately if it causes prolonged stinging, burning, itching, blemishes, or redness. It's a given that it won't be beneficial to you in any way.

Specialized Treatment for Problem Areas

We all have regions of predictive vulnerability on our faces that might require some extra attention, and they may age faster than the rest of our faces. Our genetics, the way we look when we are tired versus well rested, areas of crinkling, and the lines or creases that pop up when we make a facial expression, can all indicate these problem areas.

In addition, our relatives' skin problems can also help us to pinpoint certain skin conditions that we might be predisposed to. Some of the most common causes of concern for Level Ones are not age related. They include breakouts that follow them into adulthood; rosacea, which sometimes occurs in the twenties; dermatitis; under-eye circles and puffiness. If after three months of taking the measures described below, you still want further improvements, you might want to consider the slightly more aggressive treatments outlined in chapter 4.

CLEARING UP ACNE

It's not fair but often times we finally manage to emerge from an acne-ridden adolescence only to find that blemishes follow us into adulthood. Adult breakouts are particularly common to women in their thirties, mostly due to hormonal fluctuations, but they still can occur at any time. But while it may look the same, adult acne needs to be handled differently from the teenage variety in order to prevent the dryness and irritation that prompts skin to produce even more potentially pore-clogging sebum.

To treat acne most effectively yet gently, start out by using over-the-counter antiacne remedies that contain either exfoliating, pore-clearing salicylic acid or bacteria-banishing benzoyl peroxide. If neither works well enough independently, try using them both together. If you still aren't pleased with the results after a month, it's probably time to see a dermatologist who will prescribe the appropriate course of action for you. If you have a cyst (a painful infected nodule), it's wise to see a dermatologist as soon as possible since they generally don't respond to over the counter treatments and only get worse if left unchecked.

Prescription remedies for acne may include birth control pills (some are FDA approved to work on acne by controlling hormonal fluctuations); antibiotics to kill bacteria, such as tetracycline, doxycycline, and minocycline; topical tretinoins (retinoic acids), such as Retin-A and Differen Gel, which will help prevent blockages in the oil glands, or the antiacne drug Accutane, an oral retinoid. Here are a few tips to help you maximize any antiacne regimen, whether it is prescription or over the counter.

* **Plan ahead:** Pimples are extremely sneaky. The ones that appear next week are actually percolating today. So if you tend to get blemishes all over your face rather than in specific spots, unless directed otherwise by your doctor, stop them before they start by applying a thin layer of antiacne medication all over your face, not just on existing blemishes.

* **Look for patterns:** While breakouts may seem totally random, they actually often are "scheduled." For example, they may routinely get worse the week before your period. If this is the case, treating skin around this time can greatly reduce their severity. Stress is also a notorious acne aggravator. So if you know you are about to enter a stressful period, start applying your product before you get there.

* **Change your regimen as needed:** Since nearly all acne treatments can dry out skin, switch to a milder cleanser and/or start using oil-free moisturizer. Taking these measures is more beneficial for acne-prone skin than having to cut back on the strength or frequency of antiacne medications because of dryness.

It is understandably tempting to pop a pimple in an attempt to minimize its appearance. But this is one temptation I urge you to try your hardest to resist. When a dermatologist drains a pimple, the doctor applies downward pressure perpendicularly to the skin's surface. When people try to pop their own pimples, they usually squeeze them from the sides, a technique that inevitably backfires. The reason? Squeezing a compressible substance from the sides causes as much infection to go down deeper into the pore as is released outward. This may permanently enlarge pores and worsen infections. Meanwhile the pressure from nails can cause broken blood vessels and permanent scarring. If the temptation is just too great, try washing your face with a clean washcloth. If the pimple is ready to "pop," this is all the pressure it should need to drain. If it stubbornly refuses to budge, it's really better in the long run to just let it run its course.

CALMING ROSACEA

At Level One, sometimes what appears to be acne is actually rosacea. Though it tends to put in its first appearance in the thirties and forties, rosacea can develop at any time in varying degrees of severity. People with fair skin are more prone, and it does run in families. Rosacea's exact cause has been an endless source of debate in the medical community, but it is known to have both a bacterial and an inflammatory component. Its symptoms include diffuse redness (flushing), broken capillaries, and inflamed bumps or pimples, which is why it is often confused with acne. But conventional blemish remedies, such as benzoyl peroxide and Retin A, generally exacerbate rosacea because they provoke more inflammation, though it is possible to have both conditions simultaneously, in which case consulting a doctor as to your appropriate course of treatment is your best bet.

It is possible to control a mild case simply by limiting caffeine, alcohol (especially red wine), spicy food, and exposure to extreme temperatures. There are also many over-the-counter remedies, which are designed to reduce redness and soothe inflammation. Maintain an extremely gentle cleansing regimen and avoid alcohol-based products to help reduce the frequency and severity of flare-ups.

Angie,* twenty-four, had rosacea but was reluctant to admit it because she thought that it "only happened to old people." Before she saw me, she had had one minor outbreak and her doctor had given her a prescription for medication, which she never used. A few months later, she had a full-blown attack that she started treating with antiacne remedies, which only made things worse. After speaking in depth, we realized that her rosacea was entirely dietary related. She only had flare-ups after she ate spicy foods, which she did most of the time. Specifically, she would spice up anything she ate—even her morning eggs—and had a real penchant for Indian and Mexican cuisine. She has since eliminated spicy foods from her diet and hasn't had a problem since. But eating just one meal or even a bite of spicy food can trigger an outbreak. Ellen, thirty-three, actually had a bad attack from eating just one chip with salsa.

But if taking the above steps aren't enough to prevent and clear up rosacea eruptions, you might want to consider incorporating the more aggressive preventative and curative measures outlined in chapter 4 into your regimen. And if one or more of the following symptoms accompanies your breakouts, I suggest seeing your doctor: excessive facial or body hair growth; irregular periods; unexplained weight gain or loss; and/or excessive hair loss. These symptoms could indicate thyroid or other hormonal imbalances, such as polycystic ovary disease, which if left unchecked, can promote greater health problems and compromise fertility. Blood tests may show testosterone, prolactin, DHEA, thyroid, and

*The name has been changed.

other hormones. These symptoms may also occur as the result of the acute hormonal fluctuations associated with pregnancy, starting or stopping birth control pills, or nursing. When in doubt, see your doctor.

SOOTHING SEBORRHEIC DERMATITIS

Because it has many of the same symptoms as severely dry skin—itching, redness, flaking, and scaling—seborrheic dermatitis can be difficult to self-diagnose. But it is actually an inflammatory rash, not a condition caused by lack of moisture. Unfortunately, treating it as though it were dry skin with intense moisturization won't help it, and exfoliation only aggravates the rash. One way to distinguish seborrheic dermatitis from ordinary dryness is that it is usually localized, in particular around the sides of the nose and/or eyebrows. If this is the case, try treating the rash as it crops up with an over-the-counter 1 percent hydrocortisone cream. If the dry flakes persist, see a dermatologist to confirm your diagnosis and for a stronger or more targeted treatment.

FADING DARK CIRCLES

For the most part, dark under-eye circles in Level One are the result of lifestyle habits such as smoking, drinking too much caffeine, overindulging in alcohol, and not sleeping enough, rather than the thinning of the skin that occurs with aging. Nicotine, alcohol, and caffeine cause the capillaries to leak iron and blood cells into the under-eye area, giving it a dark appearance. In addition, lack of sleep, or extreme stress can put your body into flight or fight mode, which means your brain, like other vital organs, leaches every single molecule of oxygen it can from the blood, so a darker more deoxygenated blood flows through our veins to the other areas of the body. This dark blood is most visible in the transparent skin under our eyes and is what causes the appearance of those discolored rings.

In addition to maintaining a healthy lifestyle, keeping any allergies or sinus conditions in check can also help to reduce dark circles. Eye creams with vitamin K can heal the broken capillaries to prevent them from leaking blood into the under-eye region. Other helpful ingredients include retinoids and vitamin C (ascorbic acid), both of which will help to thicken the skin so any darkness there becomes less visible. I specifically took this multipronged approach when I formulated M.D. Skincare Lift & Lighten Cream.

Sometimes dark circles are the result of hyperpigmentation, areas of the skin that are permanently darker than the rest of the face due to sun damage, hormonal fluctuations, or genetics. Tanya, twenty-seven, for example, seemed to develop superdark circles overnight, something not uncommon for people with olive complexions. She slept well and maintained a healthy lifestyle but even so, those rings got darker and darker. That phenomenon let us rule out leaky capillaries and darkened blood flow as the cause. We had her start using an over-the-counter eye cream, which contained skin thickening ascorbic acid plus kojic acid, another lightening agent. After three months of twice daily usage, the circles were significantly lighter. She even cut down the amount of concealer she used to apply by about a third.

DEFLATING PUFFY UNDER-EYES

Pouching out of the under-eye skin can have several causes. The most common is inheriting thick or unevenly distributed fat pads in that region. This thickness can be compounded by water retention due to diet, sleeping habits, alcohol, and hormonal fluctuations (bags are often bigger right before your period when the body tends to retain more water). They can also be due to allergies and sinus conditions. When the nose or sinuses are inflamed and congested, fluid accumulates under the eyes in the fat pads.

If you have a tendency to become puffy, reduce salt intake and minimize alcohol consumption, since both salt and alcohol can make us retain excess water. Taking any allergy or sinus medication daily as directed—not just with an attack—can prevent the swelling of the nasal passages and sinuses that also can inflate the area. Sleeping on our backs as opposed to our sides or stomach, and elevating the head of the bed are other good ways to help prevent fluids from collecting and stretching out under-eye skin. Another excellent way to prevent and reduce under-eye puffiness is to do some form of cardiovascular exercise regularly, since revving up the circulatory system and sweating helps us to release excess water. In the past, many doctors advocated surgically removing the under-eye fat pads on younger women who were bothered by bags. However, if performed too early or if too much fat is removed, the under eye can look eerily hollow as we age. In addition, under-eye puffs caused by sinus and nasal congestion won't be fully flattened even if the fat pads are taken out.

One new way of thinking is to treat under-eye pouches with products that temporarily tighten the skin and liberate trapped fluid. In my experience, under-eye gels with caffeine and cucumber extract are the ones that really work. In addition, preparations with green tea extract can soothe redness and inflammation.

While many articles on the subject have advocated putting these products in the fridge to impart them with even more anti-swelling benefits, I don't find this to be the case. It may make them feel more soothing and cooling to inflamed skin but our body temperature warms them up in seconds, thus eliminating their powers of deflation. The same goes for those ubiquitous cold cucumber slices seen fairly frequently on young starlets getting Hollywood-style facials on the big screen. While they certainly can't hurt, they aren't quite cold enough and don't contain enough concentrated cucumber extract to make a real difference, though I suspect putting new slices on as soon as the old ones heat up could make them somewhat effective. Natural remedies that seem to work better include ice packs, which decrease swelling and inflammation, and frozen green or white tea bags (their tannins are a natural anti-inflammatory).

In addition, certain foods, like celery, cucumber, watermelon, parsley, and parsnip have a natural diuretic effect, which also can help reduce puffiness. However, prescription or over-the-counter diuretics should never be taken without the guidance of a physician. And one more advisory: There's that old chestnut about Preparation H being the antipuff product of choice for models at photo shoots and fashion shows. I don't know how that one got started, but that ointment is meant for only one area of the body and that isn't under our eyes.

LIGHTENING SUNSPOTS AND OTHER DISCOLORATIONS

Brown spots and freckles are actually little growths caused by cumulative sun exposure. These round sunspots are darker than the rest of our faces because they are filled with excess melanin pigment, our skin's defensive reaction to the sun. If the darkness is less freckly and more patchy and diffuse it could be melasma. Melasma usually includes dark streaks on the upper lip, forehead, or around the eyes. In addition to sun exposure, female hormones worsen melasma, especially during pregnancy (called pregnancy mask) or when taking oral contraceptives. However just being in your reproductive years is a risk factor for developing it.

The good news is that we can greatly reduce the severity of and risk for developing either condition by wearing a broad-spectrum sunblock with at least an SPF 15, sunglasses, and a wide-brimmed hat on summer days. At this level, over-the-counter bleaching—also called lightening or whitening—products with active ingredients such as ascorbic acid, combined with kojic acid or hydroquinone can do an excellent job of lightening both sunspots and melasma. I recommend using products that contain several different active ingredients, since they are generally more effective and less irritating.

All bleaching products can be harsh even when used as directed. They also cause hypersensitivity to the sun. It is an odd paradox that the key remedy for hyperpigmented skin can worsen the problem. Both irritation and photosensitivity actually can make dark spots darker and increase our chances of getting new ones. If skin becomes red and irritated from any bleaching product, cut back on its frequency of use, say from every night to every other night. Be especially diligent about wearing sunscreen and even trade up to an SPF 30 to help the lightening agents effectively do their job without exacerbating the problem.

For the best, least skin-irritating results, apply a thin amount only to dark areas at least one hour before bedtime. This will let it fully absorb into the skin so it won't slide into your eyes when you press your face into the pillow. When applying it, avoid getting it into your eyes since it will sting. As effective as some bleaching agents can be, especially stubborn sunspots may require a few sessions of laser therapy to eliminate them. For details, turn to chapter 4. Melasma, however, is exacerbated by laser treatments and so should only be treated with bleaching products.

HANDLING BROKEN CAPILLARIES

Those little red squiggles are actually misnamed—they are not so much broken capillaries, as they are extra capillaries. Our skin forms these additional blood vessels when our bodies and/or skin have been subjected to some kind of trauma so that the blood, nutrients, and oxygen it needs can be carried there to heal the damage. They are also a component of rosacea, but can be the result of any facial trauma, such as squeezing a blemish overzealously.

Extreme temperatures can also cause broken capillaries. Prolonged exposure to the excessive heat of fireplaces, steam rooms, saunas, and Jacuzzis can cause our body to create extra blood vessels to increase blood flow to help cool us off. Excessive *cold*, on the other hand, prompts our body to conserve heat internally by constricting the blood vessels on the skin's surface. Skin then becomes shortchanged of the nutrients, blood flow, and oxygen it needs to function optimally. In response to this stress, our skin produces more vessels in an attempt to supply it with what it is lacking. Limiting caffeine, alcohol, and spicy foods also may help prevent capillary formation—especially if you are genetically predisposed to rosacea. At this time, no topical product or ingredient has been proven effective at shrinking or eliminating these tiny red lines. The only way to get the job done is with a few sessions of nonablative laser treatments. See chapter 4 for more details.

STAVING OFF LINES, WRINKLES, AND SAGGING

While lines, wrinkles, and sagging are all caused by the breakdown of collagen and elastin, each problem is unique in why and when it appears. For Level One skin, you can prevent and treat all three in the same way—mostly with the collagen-building and skin-protecting measures previously described. As we age, though, each problem might require slightly different tactics.

Lines are generally the result of wear and tear to the areas of our face that are involved in its movement—its natural grooves or seams, so to speak. The best examples are the lines around our eyes and in between our brows. After years of squinting or scowling, be it in concentration, perplexity, or anger, the collagen and elastin eventually break down, resulting in creases. Wrinkles, however, occur in the areas of the face that are stationary, such as the cheeks. There's really no reason for their existence other than environmental damage and the passage of time. Sagging, on the other hand, is mostly the result of genetics. It all depends on the thickness of our skin as well as the formation of its structural proteins and connective tissue.

Believe it or not, retraining ourselves not to make some very basic facial expressions, such as scowling, can make all the difference in minimizing the appearance of lines. Whenever we feel tense or angry, if we consciously take a moment to take a few deep breaths, it will not only benefit our psyche and ability to make a clear decision, but also our skin, since it will force us to relax our facial muscles. Taking B-complex vitamins or so-called stress tabs have also been shown to ease tension.

To help prevent sagging and the appearance of deep creases in our nasolabial folds (the deep lines that run alongside the nose to the mouth), it is important to keep our weight stable and avoid dramatic weight loss past forty, which can tax our skin's elasticity and disproportionately deepen our nasolabial folds. Restrict exposure to the extreme collagen- and elastin-decomposing heat of saunas, steam rooms, and Jacuzzis as well as limit the amount of high impact exercise. While such exercise may benefit our hearts, it can cause the fat pads to slide south and collagen and elastin to break down. Quit smoking, so the face no longer receives secondhand smoke, which produces free radicals—another major offensive play.

The best news of all? Putting on a little weight can definitely plump up a sagging and/or drawn-looking face as well as push out lines and wrinkles.

At Level One, the important thing to remember (but not get hung up on) is that at this phase in your skin's life cycle, beauty is really only skin deep; deep down below its surface, it is starting to age. But the good news is that you can both forestall and reverse the mechanisms that are already at play. Prevention here is clearly defined: You should focus on collagen production and defend yourself from further damage from the sun and free radicals.

4
Level Two

ACTIVE REPAIR AND PROTECTION

I f you scored Level Two (a range of 35–46), now is your greatest opportunity to take charge of your skin and postpone the signs of aging. Your skin is at a very dynamic phase of its life cycle right now and still maintains many of its defense and regenerative abilities, so your face will respond all the more favorably to any course of action your choose. You also have an enormous opportunity to take good, solid preventative measures that will, without question, prolong your skin's youthful appearance. In terms of age, my Level Two patients are generally in their early thirties to forties and are starting to have some concerns about their appearance. It could be sheet marks that linger longer than they used to, sunspots that don't fade after the summer, fine lines around the eyes, and/or a furrow between the brows. Perhaps there's a crinkling effect in the skin when you pinch it and in some places when you don't, slight sagging, visible red blood vessels (broken capillaries), more pronounced acne or chicken pox scars, and/or enlarged pores. This is because the aging that had been going on previously only under your skin has now started to surface.

As previously discussed, the level of your skin is not just age dependent. If you are generally happy with the way you look, Level Two measures will almost certainly give you all the improvements you desire whether you are in your thirties, forties, fifties, sixties, or seventies. These strategies also encompass good basic skin-care habits that women of all ages can combine with the measures listed in the previous chapter (Level One) and in chapter 8 to use as the building blocks of their regimen.

The science of antiaging has made leaps and bounds over the last decade and continues to discover better, faster, less invasive, and easier ways to turn back the clock and keep it there. The advent of nonablative (no injury) lasers, light acid peels, hyaluronic acid–based fillers, and the refinement of Botox injections all provide exciting and amazingly effective ways to keep your skin looking its best with little or no recovery time and are nearly tailor-made to *your* skin's present condition. If these treatments are coupled with solid daily skin-care habits and a healthy lifestyle, they will continue to give you stunning results as your skin matures.

The most important thing to remember at this level is not to do anything drastic or permanent. Procedures such as permanent fillers, surgical implants, or a face-lift, simply may not look good over time as your face matures and changes shape. And because you are, for the most part, happy with your appearance, a dramatic change is not really what you are looking for right now— and maybe not ever.

For now, temporary is truly the only way to go. Start your antiaging regimen off with the least aggressive at-home procedures and over-the-counter products. Then you can gradually work your way up the ladder in terms of aggressiveness to prescription products and in-office treatments, if need be. My other caveat, which rings true for all levels, is to resist the temptation to be the first kid on your block to try any new ingredient or procedure. There are enough antiaging treatments that have been proven by good solid science to be safe and effective that you never need to put yourself at risk for something that hasn't.

The Basics

While this chapter will offer slightly more aggressive alternatives to intensively treat specific areas of vulnerability, a sound daily skin-care regimen is still the cornerstone of beautiful skin. All the high-tech ingredients and treatments in the world will never be able to achieve their full benefits if your skin isn't in the best condition it can possibly be. Here are a few simple additions and adjustments to the daily skin-care regimen discussed in chapter 3. Your basic routine will still involve cleansing, exfoliating, building collagen and elastin stores, and paying extra attention to your undereye area, while defending your skin against the sun and free radicals. However, in this chapter, we will intensify your daily defensive measures while adding in some reparative ones. These small changes will go far in helping you get and maintain sensational-looking skin.

1. JUST ADD WATER: MOISTURIZING TWICE A DAY

It's no secret that water plays an important part in our well-being. It comprises nearly two-thirds of our body weight and at least that much of each of our vital organs as well as our muscles. Water is also a key ingredient in radiant, healthy-looking skin and helps it to maintain a certain degree of plumpness—in this instance, a very good thing. When skin is plump, lines and wrinkles are less apparent and enlarged pores look smaller.

Your skin is actually designed to draw in water and trap it there. This capability is due to sodium hyaluronate, a complex molecule found naturally in the fluid between the skin cells, which can hold up to 100 times its own weight in water. Also known as hyaluronic acid, this virtual moisture magnet first attracts then locks water into skin. As we age, our skin's overall water content and its hyaluronic acid stores both decline. Menopause also reduces skin water content due to reduced estrogen (see chapter 6). But bringing back some of what time takes away is simple enough— just use a moisturizer twice a day.

A moisturizer works in two phases: It first delivers water to the skin and then seals it in with an emollient ingredient, such as oil. Even if you have oily skin, you can still benefit from adding water to your skin (also called hydrating) with a moisturizer because oil (your skin's lipids) and water actually serve two completely different functions. Water keeps the skin supple, while lipids are the sealants that trap it there. If you have oily skin, using an oil-free moisturizer will still increase skin plumpness and vibrancy due to its water content, but won't clog pores or cause blemishes because it lacks oil. Products that contain hyaluronic acid are particularly effective for oily complexions and, actually, a great choice for all skin types. When applied topically, hyaluronic acid works very much the same way as it does internally—it attracts water and then traps it inside the skin so that no extra sealant (emollient) is necessary.

2. BOLSTER YOUR NATURAL DEFENSES:
THE BENEFITS OF RETINOL AND GENISTEIN TO PROTECT AND BUILD COLLAGEN

Antioxidants such as green tea extract, vitamins C and E and lycopene continue to play an important part in your collagen-protecting, free radical-destroying routine. But free radicals aren't the only collagen chompers. Your skin actually contains naturally occurring enzymes that erode it, as well. As we mature, these enzymes become stronger than the mechanisms in our skin that combat them. Retinol has been found to combat these destructive forces, giving us just one more reason to include it in our daily skin-care regimens. But a newer ingredient with promising research behind it may prove to be as, if not even more, effective. Genistein, a component of soy extract, isolated by Dr. Genistein in Switzerland, has been shown to block and diminish these collagen-destroying enzymes considerably. The best part? It is completely nonirritating and so works beautifully with all other antiaging ingredients. Still, genistein, a nonprescription ingredient, should be considered an addition to your regimen rather than a retinol replacement. The more ways you can defend yourself against collagen breakdown, the better.

3. REV UP CELL RENEWAL:
EXFOLIATE WITH LIGHT PEELS

Another surefire way to keep skin glowing and smooth is to exfoliate daily to prevent the buildup of dulling dead skin cells and other debris. While your cell turnover starts to decline at thirty, it continues to slow down with the years. Consider exfoliation the key to keeping this function alive and kicking. In addition to giving you a smoother and more radiant complexion, consistently increasing cell turnover may have the added benefit of stimulating collagen production. Repeated exfoliation and the reduction in dead skin cells that results are believed to rev up the machinery that helps renew the skin. Take men who shave (an excellent means of exfoliation), for example. The lower part of their face, the area that they most commonly shave, actually ages better than their upper half, which for the most part, has never seen a razor.

If you haven't already embarked on the basic skin-sloughing steps outlined in the preceding chapter, your skin would definitely benefit from trying them now. If you have already incorporated these steps and are happy with the results, don't change a thing. If you are finding that you need a little extra help, however, you can kick your exfoliating efforts up a notch with light acid (also called superficial chemical) peels.

The word "peel" is actually a misnomer. In reality, a peel is a two-step process with no actual peeling involved. The first step is to swab a mixture of exfoliating acids on skin to remove the dead cells and other skin-dulling debris. The second step is to apply a liquid base that neutralizes the acids and conditions the skin. In addition to stimulating collagen production, which will soften lines and wrinkles, firm skin, and even our skin tone, repetitive peels can also help to reduce pore size, fade discolorations, improve rosacea, as well as to treat and prevent acne.

In peels, it is not only the exfoliating act of the acids that's firing up collagen formation, but the PH fluctuation the skin experiences as it goes from acidic to neutral. I've coined the term *Phlux* because it is such a powerful action. Phlux appears to be an even bigger catalyst in cell turnover and creates an extra benefit to conventional exfoliation with a lotion or cream alone. The more potent the ingredient that exfoliates and the more dramatic the PH fluctuation, the more revved up your skin becomes to replace and renew the skin. As seductive as this concept may be—the deeper the peel, the more collagen you produce—don't let it sway you into automatically assuming a deep peel is your best course of action. While deep peels produce more collagen than light peels, this production is in direct response to the damage the peel inflicts to your skin. Medium and deep peels are actually controlled injuries to your skin and stimulate collagen synthesis in much the same way that a deep cut or burn promotes scar tissue as part of the healing process. And while that damage does come with the benefit of enhanced collagen production and so can smooth away deeper lines and darker sunspots, it also carries some risks, which we will discuss in Levels Three and Four (chapters 5 and 6).

But the good news is that when light peels are performed on a regular basis, they can have very similar benefits to deep or medium peels without the potential side effects. I have consistently found that the cumulative results of repetitive light peels can exceed those of medium peels and come close to those of deep peels without any of the associated risks.

The safest and most effective light peels contain a variety of acids so that each one can be used in lower and less irritating concentrations. I developed the M.D. Skincare Alpha Beta Peel ten years ago in response to the harsh glycolic acid peels that were currently the rage in the dermatological community. (See "A Series of Alpha Beta Peels" in the photo section.) I was frustrated because I found these procedures to be overly aggressive without achieving the desired results. The Alpha Beta Peel is available in home, spa, and medical grades. All of the versions contain salicylic, malic, citric, lactic, and glycolic acids, as well as soothing green tea extract, which also protects against free radicals, and retinol, which further stimulates collagen synthesis, strengthens connective tissue and inhibits the enzymes in our skin that degrade collagen. I have recently incorporated genistein into them, as well.

Andrea, thirty-eight, is practically a poster child for light acid peels and talks about them to anyone who'll listen. She had always had nice skin, the result of limited sun exposure when she was a child and good genetics. She came to me in her early thirties originally for removal of a mole, which actually turned out to be precancerous, but then started asking me how she could keep her skin looking good longer and maybe even make it a little better (she had a slight tendency toward rosacea and some enlarged pores on her nose). We started her on in-office peels once a month, using the daily at-home Alpha Beta Peel, and wearing sunscreen on a daily basis, plus topical vitamin C product at night. After just a few months on this regimen, she says perfect strangers were asking her the brand name of her makeup when she wasn't wearing any and that people are shocked when she tells them she's been married for twelve years because they generally assume she's around twenty-eight.

Nancy, thirty-six, is also a huge Alpha Beta Peel fan. Even though she had been careful of the sun her whole life, when she hit her early thirties, her pores got bigger, she had diffuse crinkling all over her face, and her skin just wasn't as tight as it used to be. She felt that all these things made her look older than she actually was. Within months of doing monthly in-office peels and using at-home peels on a daily basis, she had completely arrested and diminished the crinkling and regained much of her loss in firmness. She was and continues to be thrilled.

I can name hundreds of patients of all ages and mind-sets that have had similar experiences with light peels combined with good daily skin-care habits. With just a few simple products, these women have shaved off years from their appearances. And by continuing these healthy tendencies, they will maintain their youthful complexions longer and age far more gracefully than they would have otherwise—even if they never take more aggressive measures.

Peels 101

Peels are available in three depths: light, medium, and deep. For Level Two skin, light peels should be sufficient. They are the least invasive and cause virtually no redness, swelling, or irritation, though they may sting slightly upon application and result in some minor flaking for a day or so afterward. People with excessively dry skin might find them to be more uncomfortable and that they can make their skin even drier. If this is the case, I suggest cutting back on your frequency—say two to three times a week for a home peel instead of on a daily basis. The results of light peels are cumulative—but amazing nonetheless. Your skin will look better and better and stay looking that way longer over time as you continue to perform them. (See photo section, page 4).

Light peels are available in three strengths:

Home: These peels contain the lowest concentration of acids as governed by law and so are the mildest. They are a perfect way to introduce your skin to this type of treatment to gauge how it will react. You even might find that they give you enough of an improvement that you don't need to trade up to a stronger version. Use as directed, up to once a day.

Spa: This treatment is infused with nonprescription concentrations of acids but is more potent than the home version and so is administered less frequently—once or twice a month or so—to achieve visible benefits. When they are applied by a trained professional—make sure yours is—they can yield immediate results that can last up to a month. The end benefits can be enhanced and maintained with home peels.

Medical: This variation contains prescription strengths of acids and can only be performed by a trained medical professional. It may sting a bit more than the other two versions but the sensation is generally slight and extremely short-lived. These peels impart the most immediate and dramatic improvements. Your skin will be more radiant, smooth, even, and softer immediately. Over time and with repeated application, your skin also will be firmer, your pore size reduced, your breakouts lessened, and your lines and wrinkles softened. Depending on the condition of their skin and their genetic predispositions, some of my patients get in-office peels as frequently as once a month. Getting medical peels more often than that is usually overkill and not necessarily more beneficial to the skin. Your doctor can help you develop a peel regimen best suited to your skin type and needs. Again, using home peels on a regular basis will extend and enhance your results. (See "A Series of Alpha Beta Peels" in the photo section.)

4. INCREASE COLLAGEN AND ELASTIN PRODUCTION WITH VITAMIN C, GENISTEIN, ANTIOXIDANTS, AND RETINOIDS

Build, build, build—collagen and elastin that is. As discussed, they are the key support structures of skin and unfortunately they continue to decline in both quality and quantity as we age. In addition to peels and the products outlined in the last chapter, modern science has discovered many revolutionary and noninvasive ways to jump-start the collagen-producing machinery to help keep your skin smooth and youthful looking and even reverse many of the signs of premature aging. If you haven't already started using the basic collagen-boosting, over-the-counter vitamin C- and retinol-based products discussed in chapter 3, your skin would benefit greatly from trying them now. They not only will give you positive results today but will also prevent future damage. If you have been using basic collagen-building products and are happy with the results, keep up the good work. If, however, you have incorporated them into your daily routine, and you're still noticing some unwelcome changes to your skin, you can talk to your dermatologist about using retinoids. FDA-approved, prescription-strength retinoids can promote collagen content in the skin and inhibit the skin's collagen-degrading enzymes. Renova, Retin-A, and Tazarotene are the most commonly prescribed brands of wrinkle fighters. But while they are often considered to be interchangeable, in my experience, it turns out that Renova is perferable. Retin-A is better at fighting acne, but it does work on lines and wrinkles as well.

Renova is available as moisturizing cream in a variety of strengths. If you choose to incorporate this product into your regimen, start out with the mildest version possible and gradually work your way up to a stronger one, if necessary. Because Retin-A and Renova are more potent than retinol, their nonprescription counterpart, they can cause irritation and increased sensitivity to other active ingredients and to the sun. Still, they can yield beneficial results. Wearing an SPF 30 will help prevent further damage and worsening of any damage you already have. If you find that retinoids are irritating to the point that they are preventing you from using your other antiaging remedies, I recommend either using your retinoid cream less frequently (every other day instead of on a daily basis, for example), trying a milder, more moisturizing version, or trading back down to retinol, the nonprescription strength. It's better to combat the aging process from all angles with a variety of different ingredients (antioxidants, exfoliating acids, vitamin C, etc.), instead of relying on a single ingredient that tackles only one aspect.

The (No-Injury) Laser's Edge

A Safe and Effective Collagen Boost

I have found there to be enormous preventative as well as line-erasing and skin-firming benefits from performing a series of non-ablative (i.e., noninvasive) laser treatments on my patients of all levels, particularly around the eyes and mouth and on crinkled areas, and extensive research supports my experiences. (See "Noninvasive Laser for Wrinkles" in the photo section.)

The beams from the no-injury Smooth Beam, N-Lite, and Cool Touch lasers spur collagen production without having to injure the skin to do so. There is no "resurfacing" per se but rather a heat-induced stimulation to the cells that create collagen, called fibroblasts, which over time thickens the underlying collagen structure—skin is literally being built up from the inside out. With the more aggressive ablative lasers, which we will discuss in Levels Three and Four (chapters 5 and 6), the surface of the skin is removed. It is this controlled injury that prompts the fibroblasts to produce more collagen (see medium and deep lasers, pages 65–66).

Most noninvasive laser procedures are performed with topical anesthetic cream applied at least ten minutes before treatment. Laser treatments may cause some minimal but tolerable discomfort. Skin in the surrounding area may be somewhat red for twelve to twenty-four hours and faint markings in the treated areas can remain visible for a day or two afterward, but they can be easily concealed with makeup. Other than that, there are no other side effects to this treatment. Noninvasives are also wonderfully effective in minimizing acne scars. I typically administer a series of three to five treatments one month apart. Results are usually visible after three months. You and your doctor will decide the best course of action for you, based on your skin's condition and the results you want. Though the improvements from noninvasive lasers may be subtler than those from deeper laser resurfacing, they can be extremely gratifying and permanent, nonetheless, and their preventative value is unquestionable for areas of vulnerability, such as lines in the crow's-feet area, which you may have a genetic predisposition toward developing and/or are starting to become visible, especially when you smile.

Even with a good skin-care regimen that included monthly in-office and daily at-home peels, vitamin C, and sunscreen, Claire, thirty-six, was starting to get faint lines around her eyes when she wasn't smiling. Afraid of needles, there was no way she was going to give Botox a shot. Instead, we did a course of three Smooth Beam treatments, one month apart. Three months later people started asking her if she had just come back from vacation because she looked so well rested, and a few close friends wanted to know if she had had her eyes "done." The collagen stores that she has laid in as a result of the treatments not only make her skin look better today but will also help to prevent more premature aging later on. (See "Noninvasive Lasers for Wrinkles" in the photo section.)

5. REMEMBER YOUR NECK AND CHEST:
TREATING THEM AS YOU WOULD YOUR FACE

My Level Two patients frequently come to me saying that their necks and chests look older than the rest of them. And very often that can be the case. The skin in both areas seems to take the brunt of cumulative sun exposure and seems to be more genetically predisposed to becoming the worse for the wear as a result.

Returning your décolletage to its former smoother, clearer state is completely feasible, though—you just have to apply the same good skin-care habits to these areas as you do to your face. And if you have smooth skin in these regions now, it's a great time to start giving them, as well as your hands, which can start to become problematic over the next five years, a little extra attention to ward off future problems. Sunscreen, vitamin C, retinol, multiacids, and antioxidants all can be easily incorporated into your daily after-bath or after-shower regimen. Using at-home body peels up to once a day and getting spa or medical-grade body peels as directed by your esthetician or dermatologist are also excellent preventative and positive measures.

In general, products formulated for the body have stronger concentrations of active ingredients, since the chest, especially, is usually less sensitive than the face and requires a little more oomph in the treatment department. It's fine to use facial products there, but they may not be as effective as those created specifically for the body. Using body products on the face, though, is generally not advisable since it can cause irritation and breakouts. Your neck is the transitional area between your face and chest and so some experimentation may be required to gauge whether its sensitivity is more like your face or the rest of your body. One more caveat: To date, no laser, noninvasive or otherwise, has been developed to safely and effectively treat wrinkles of the neck and chest.

Food for Thought

Does Microdermabrasion Boost Collagen Production?

A mainstay of many spas and estheticians, this system is composed of a compressor and a suction pump that work in unison to project steril aluminum oxide crystals onto the skin with a controllable intensity. Microdermabrasion simultaneously exfoliates and then "vacuums" up the dead skin cells and other complextion-dulling debris. Like a facial, this treatment can make skin smoother, softer, clearer looking, and minimize the appearance of enlarged pores and acne scars. But it is sometimes marketed as a way to help synthesize collagen. Many practitioners recommend a series of five to ten treatments to accomplish this. But reputable studies have shown that microdermabrasion has an extremely minor impact on collagen production and whatever small collagen-stimulating effect it does have is maxed out after just two treatments.

Customizing Your Daily Regimen

Avoiding irritation and inflammation is a high priority when using many different types of ingredients and procedures. It is often necessary to tweak your regimen based on the season, your travel schedule, and whether you are taking any medications that affect your hormonal balance. Irritation is not only uncomfortable but can also accelerate the aging process. The reason? The more irritation you experience, the more your skin produces free radicals. This means you might actually be aging your skin despite, or rather because of, your antiaging regimen!

Two to three minutes of tingling, not burning, is what I would call acceptable irritation because it means that your skin is accommodating to the ingredient. Any greater discomfort is reason enough to back off. Immediately discontiune any product that outright burns, causes itching, flaking, or redness.

There are a few ways to minimize reactivity to antiaging ingredients:

Change cleansers: A real downfall to any skin-care routine is a harsh facial wash. If your skin feels dry and tight a few minutes after toweling off, it's time to trade down to a milder cleanser. You may then find that the ingredients that used to sting no longer do.

Use less: Try cutting whatever quantity you were applying in half. You might simply have been overwhelming your skin with more than it needed. While it may seem logical, more product won't give you faster or better results.

Adjust your frequency: If you are using all of your products twice a day, try applying some in the morning and some at night, or try alternating days.

Start over: If the above measures don't seem to be helping, take a break from all active antiaging and acne-fighting ingredients (except sunscreen) for three days or more to let your skin rest. Once it has recovered, reintroduce yourself to one ingredient at a time. You might, for example, start your vitamin C product for one week; then add your home peels for a week; and lastly add your retinol product into the mix. If all of a sudden your skin becomes irritated, you'll know that the ingredient you just added back in is too strong for you. If this is the case, you can either reduce its strength or the frequency with which you apply it, or both.

Know when to say when: If backing down isn't helping, stop. You may be one of the people who simply can't tolerate a certain ingredient. But there are more than enough other ones out there that will work for you.

Specialized Treatment for Problem Areas

Your specific areas of predictive vulnerability might require extra measures. Your genetics, the way you look when you are tired versus well rested, any areas of crinkling, and the lines or creases that pop up when you make a facial expression can all indicate the parts of your face that may age faster than the rest of you. Even if you can't see these problems today, taking extra precautions, in addition to good daily skin-care habits, can significantly prolong your years without them. And if you have the faintest hint of any concern, you have a huge opportunity to reverse the damage and prevent it from getting worse. If you are just noticing these changes now, start treating them with the strategies discussed in chapter 3. If after three months you still want further improvements, you can try trading up to the more potent products and procedures below. Should any problem really stand out to you, you might want to consider taking the slightly more aggressive measures outlined in chapter 5 (Level 3).

IMPROVING THE UNDER-EYE REGION

In addition to the lifestyle habits we discussed in chapter 3 that can cause under-eye capillaries to leak blood and create dark circles, another factor can come into play now. As you get into your thirties and beyond, the skin under the eyes, which is thinner than the rest of the face to begin with, starts to thin out even more, making any discoloration underneath more visible. Healing the broken blood vessels with a vitamin K product is still an effective means to reduce the appearance of dark rings, especially when combined with bleaching agents like kojic and ascorbic acids. But building up collagen stores in this region is also advisable since it will help thicken the skin so the circles become less apparent. If you've already tried the over-the-counter collagen builders discussed in chapter 3, pages 37–38, and still seek further improvements after six weeks, you can climb up the ladder in terms of aggressiveness by adding light acid peels into your at-home skin-care regimen. The next step would be to start getting spa or medical grade peels and then perhaps a series of noninvasive laser treatments. Lastly, you can talk to your dermatologist about using Renova or Tazarotene. Because all of these courses of action enhance collagen production, they also can have a tightening effect on under-eye puffs. These remedies are also extremely effective in easing and preventing fine lines in the crow's-feet area. But if the lines are more pronounced even when you are just smiling, you might want to consider Botox injections. (See "Preventing and Smoothing Out Lines," page 79.)

Each one of these treatments can also reap excellent benefits on its own, but in my experience, combining a few of them is more effective, since each works a bit differently and may tackle a different aspect of the problem.

FADING SUNSPOTS AND OTHER DISCOLORATIONS

Now might be the time you begin to notice that those little brown spots that appear every summer don't disappear in late fall like they used to; plus you might have more than ever before. It also might be the time when melasma puts in its first appearance or becomes darker if it made its debut in your twenties. While they do take time and patience, skin-bleaching products offer a safe, easy, and noninvasive way to lighten these discolorations. The one caveat? Bleaching products can increase photosensitivity and irritate skin, which can actually intensify the darkness in a hyperpigmented area. But by being vigilant in your use of sunscreen and conservative in how often and how much of the cream you apply, after three to six months, these spots will be much lighter.

If you haven't already, start by using the over-the-counter bleaching agents. If after several months, you still aren't happy with the results, you can trade up to a prescription version. In my experience, prescription creams that I personally formulate for my patients that contain 4 percent hydroquinone combined with kojic acid work the best. Because bleaching creams increase your skin's sensitivity to the sun, it's best to use them at night. Apply to completely dry skin one hour before bed so the cream can't slide into your eyes when your face presses against the pillow. If you have any pinkness or irritation, take a step back. Stop using the product and other active ingredients for three or so days to let your skin rest. Once it has recovered, start using the cream a few nights a week, gradually building up to every other night and then to every night if your skin tolerates it without irritation. If it can't, no worries. You can still achieve some benefits by applying a prescription-bleaching product even just two nights a week, though it will take longer.

Any especially stubborn sunspots (called solar lentigines) can be wiped out with one to three sessions with a YAG or ruby laser. These lasers work by targeting and then destroying darker pigment in the skin. As with the nonablative laser treatments that boost collagen production, a topical numbing cream is applied before the procedure is performed so that the treatment causes only a slight amount of discomfort. Small scabs most likely will appear immediately afterward, but they usually fall off in just a few days. Other than that, there is no downtime, though lasered skin is especially sensitive to the sun and so you might require a higher SPF than you normally might wear. (An SPF 30 is recommended.)

While sunspots are great candidates for YAG or ruby lasers, melasma should never be treated with laser therapy. The injury and trauma it causes the skin, though minor and controlled, just provokes it to produce more pigment in defense.

Stacey, thirty-four, a smoker who grew up on the Jersey shore, came to me with sunspots and lines around her mouth. Believe it or not, even though she smoked, she was also a triathlete, who regularly runs marathons. She is extremely determined but also deeply critical of herself. When I told her that smoking caused and intensified the lines around her mouth, she quit smoking cold turkey. From there on in, the lines didn't get any worse, but she wanted them to significantly improve. We did a series of Smooth Beam treatments on them. In the meantime, we also did two sessions with the YAG to remove her sunspots. Gradually, she became happier and happier with the way she looked, but she became completely satisfied only after seeing the results of a consistent and solid skin-care regimen that included topical vitamin C, sunscreen, and at-home peels. (See photo section, pages 5 and 8, for results of YAG and Smooth Beam lasers.)

ERASING BROKEN CAPILLARIES

Zapping visible blood vessels is trickier than getting rid of brown spots and may take longer, but three to five sessions with a nonablative Iriderm Diode Laser can fade, shrink, and even wipe them out completely. A topical numbing cream is applied beforehand so there is only slight discomfort and, except for the possibility of some mild bruising, there is no downtime. When tackling extremely small areas, such as a tiny broken capillary, it's important that the hand piece of the laser have a super narrow opening—about the size of a ball point pen—so that it emits the finest beam of light possible. Lasers with wider openings that give off bigger beams of light, such as pulse-dye lasers, can increase the potential of overlapping—when the laser passes over the same area more than once. Overlapping, also known as doubling up, can create what the dermatological community refers to as the Swiss cheese effect—areas that are whiter than the rest of the skin because their blood flow has been destroyed by excessive lasering. The chest is particularly prone to this condition.

CALMING ROSACEA

Many women in their late thirties and early forties contract rosacea for the first time. And women who've had it in their twenties often find this condition worsens with age. If you are just experiencing it at this level, it is still possible to keep it at bay with lifestyle changes and over-the-counter remedies. If you have been adhering to that regimen for at least a month and you are not achieving visible results, you can speak to your doctor about prescription topical and oral antibiotics and light acid peels. Oral medications such as tetracycline, doxycycline and minocycline, all have been proven to keep rosacea's bacterial component under control and also seem to have an anti-inflammatory benefit. Topical products such as metronidazole and clindamycin work in much the same way. As discussed, acne fighters, such as benzoyl peroxide and retinoids may be extremely irritating to rosacea. Light peels help to keep the skin antiseptic and combat bacteria. Several treatments with a pulsed-dye laser or intense pulsed light therapy, and other noninvasive treatments that target hemoglobin in the bloodstream, can help to eradicate the diffuse redness that can accompany the condition. Diode and Iriderm lasers can zap the streaky capillaries. No laser treatment, however, is appropriate for rosacea's inflammatory bumps or pimples.

SHRINKING ENLARGED PORES

As the quality and quantity of collagen declines over time, even our pores aren't as firm as they used to be. So any debris, makeup, or excess sebum that gets lodged there can stretch out your pores beyond a point where they can shrink back. Keeping skin clean and well exfoliated and removing your makeup every night are simple, easy ways to help reduce pore size and prevent enlargement in the first place. In addition, anything that builds collagen and firms skin, such as light acid peels, vitamin C products, retinol, and antioxidants will help keep pores tighter and less likely to stretch out.

Lasers 101

While the general public believes that lasers are pretty much all the same, it turns out that they are highly specialized in their abilities. Do not believe claims that any one laser is capable of removing sunspots, erasing broken capillaries, reducing hair growth, and increasing collagen production. Different lasers specifically designed to tackle one particular issue perform optimally. And any laser treatment or series of treatments is no substitute for any of the other antiaging practices and topical ingredients.

MINIMIZING ACNE AND CHICKEN POX SCARS

Very often acne scars that were never really noticed before start to bother my Level Two patients. It's not that they've appeared for the first time, it's just that as the quality and quantity of our collagen diminishes with age, any depressions in our face appear deeper and any elevations look thicker. Any treatments that enhance collagen production, such as peels, vitamin C, lasers, and retinol, can help thicken skin to make all scars look less visible. I've also had enormous success with treating depressed scars with injectible fillers. (See "Plumping Up Creases, Wrinkles, and Depressions," page 84–89.)

PREVENTING AND SMOOTHING OUT LINES

Botox injections, which have been widely publicized and written about in both the beauty and scientific press, are truly one of the most revolutionary antiaging procedures the medical community has ever discovered. Botox is the highly purified version of the same substance that if ingested in much larger amounts can cause botulism. But Botox used cosmetically does not cause botulism because it is injected directly into facial muscles (and does not enter the bloodstream) and is used in minuscule quantities per treatment.

Botox was originally used by ophthalmologists to relieve eye spasms, cross-eyes, and facial tics, and doctors noticed that it resulted in a pleasant side effect of diminished lines in their patients who used it. Botox is no experimental procedure; it has truly stood the test of time. The FDA approved it in 1989 for ophthalmologic purposes and then later on to treat certain neurological disorders. It has been cosmetically used with great success for the last twelve years and was FDA approved in 2002 to treat the facial lines that result from muscle contractions. If you start Botox treatments just as fine lines are beginning to appear and continue to undergo them as you age, you can absolutely prevent select expression lines from forming. (See photo section, pages 6 and 8.)

It typically takes around seven days to see Botox's full benefits and results are temporary, approximately four months. So if you aren't happy with the way you look afterward, you will return to your un-Botoxed appearance in just a short while. A topical numbing cream can be applied beforehand, based on your preference and your tolerance of needles. After the procedure, you should avoid lying down flat for four hours and skip exercising that day to prevent migration into unwanted areas. Other than the possibility of some slight temporary bruising, there are no side effects. Because the FDA prohibits conducting studies on pregnant women (as it should) the effects of Botox on a fetus are unknown, so this treatment should not be performed on pregnant women.

While it is not suitable for some parts of the face or on lines that aren't the result of wear and tear, Botox is wonderfully versatile and can be used to treat and/or prevent lines that appear only when you make a facial expression and the faint expression lines that remain even when your face is relaxed. (See photo section, pages 3, 6, and 8.) Botox can even reduce deeply entrenched expression lines that have been there for quite some time—though an injectible filler also may be required for optimum results. (See "Plumping Up Creases, Wrinkles, and Depressions" pages 84–89.)

After Stephanie, thirty-seven, had gained and then lost her twenty-five pounds of pregnancy weight, she started to notice lines around her eyes and in between her brows, plus some sagging. Her mother had recently had a face-lift and since Stephanie didn't like its results, she was determined to do what she could then and there to start turning back the clock. We started her off using peels on a regular basis to help address the sagging and to refresh her skin's texture. Then we administered Botox to the lines around her eyes and in between her brows as needed. She went from looking tired all the time to looking really, really good. Intervening at this early age might also prevent her from ever even being a candidate for a face-lift.

Because Botox is a muscle immobilizer, you should make sure your physician is highly experienced and skilled at administering it. There is an artistry involved in the technique. A mere ¼ to ½ inch difference in the placement site of a Botox injection can make a huge difference in the wrinkle correction and natural appearance of your face. Here are some potential risks you should be aware of and discuss with your doctor:

* If Botox is injected too close to the outer part of the brow toward the temple, it might prevent or hinder opening that eye fully.

* If too much is placed in the forehead and/or it is injected too far down, it can give a heavy look to the brow and/or make the eyelids look droopy.

* The broadness of your smile may be compromised if Botox is injected too far down along the eyes to correct crow's-feet.

* If you already have lax skin on the upper lid, then you will be more prone to drooping eyelids than if you don't. If this is the case, your doctor needs to use less Botox than usual and inject it higher up in the forehead. It may not last as long as the average and you may get somewhat less of a correction, but it's a compromise worth making so you don't create sagging upper eyelids.

* If too much is injected into the center portion of the brow, closer to the nose, it can cause what is called the wicked-looking Diablo Effect. The outer brow shoots up to the side while the front and center portions remain motionless.

* Botoxing the lines or wrinkles on the sides of the nose that are exacerbated by facial contractions

(I call them bunny lines) can give the face a less pinched and drawn appearance. But if too much is injected or is placed too far down, you can lose your natural smile, since the Cupid's bow region of the upper lip can become paralyzed. When this happens, it is only possible to smile with the outer portions of the upper lip. This is why so many young Hollywood starlets now seem to have such strange smiles.

BOTOX CHEAT SHEET

These Botox tips are not as complicated as they may sound. When you are interviewing a potential dermatologist about receiving Botox injections, just make sure you tell him that you want to preserve the natural architecture of your face and that you *don't* want:

* The opening of your eyes to be affected
* Your brows to slope downward or shoot up
* Heaviness in the brows
* Any drooping of the upper eyelids
* Your smile to be compromised.

I've read in the consumer press that if you use Botox long enough, you eventually won't need it as often, or even at all, because your muscles eventually will atrophy. Conversely, I've also read that over time, people can build up immunity to Botox so its results won't last as long and you eventually will need more frequent injections. But in all my years of administering it, I honestly can say that I have found neither of these scenarios to be the case.

Food For Thought

Is There a Botox Replacement?

Botox in a bottle: Wouldn't it be wonderful if you could get all of Botox's proven line-relaxing benefits without the sting of a needle? That is exactly the thought that's been on the minds of many cosmetics companies. Over the last few years, many of them have been introducing creams and lotions purported to have similar line-easing effects when applied topically. While I am not familiar with all of them (there seems to be a new one marketed every month), I do know that some of these therapies incorporate heavy-metal oxides, which could minimally reduce the muscle contractions that cause the facial movements that create creases. So it is conceivable that they could very temporarily relax superficial lines. But overall my patients who tried these products, which are often expensive, have been dissatisfied. More research needs to be done to find the ingredients that can provide profound and long-lasting improvements. As an addition to your regimen, these creams can offer some benefits, but they are not a replacement for your basic antiaging regimen and certainly lack Botox's proven abilities. The one caveat? In order to be effective, many of these preparations contain a high concentration of heavy-metal oxides, which can leave behind a white, powdery residue.

Myobloc, Botox's fraternal twin? We all had high hopes for Myobloc, a purified form of Botulinum Toxin Type B. (Botox is the purified form of Botulinum Toxin Type A.) It was supposed to act faster and last longer, which would make it less expensive over the long term, since fewer shots per year would be required to maintain its results. Sounds too good to be true, right? Well, yes and no. Myobloc does, in fact, act faster than Botox—it takes full effect in a couple of days as opposed to Botox's seven. So it's ideal if you want more instant gratification; for example, if you have a special occasion in less than a week. However, in my experience Myobloc does wear off faster. How much faster? That varies from person to person. For some, it's a matter of weeks, which makes Botox a more cost-effective option for those patients.

PLUMPING UP CREASES, WRINKLES, AND DEPRESSIONS WITH INJECTIBLE FILLERS

As recently as five years ago, dermatologists could only use fat and bovine collagen injections to temporarily plump up wrinkled or sunken areas and add fullness to a drawn-looking face. Fortunately over the past few years, new options have been joining their ranks—many with extremely exciting results and the research to back them up. It is important when considering which one to use that you don't take a chance on something being marketed as "brand new." There are enough treatments that have been proven to be safe and effective, making it completely unnecessary for you to put yourself at risk.

When you are evaluating your options, as a Level Two patient, *temporary* should be your mantra. There are more permanent fillers on the market, which may seem tempting because they are more cost and time effective since they require fewer injections over the course of your lifetime. But your face is still changing, and there is no guarantee how it will age around anything foreign that has been implanted in it. Plus, if you decide later on in life that you do want to get plastic surgery, your once natural-looking permanent filler may not look that way once your skin is pulled tightly over it. I will outline the more permanent options

The Four Skin Levels

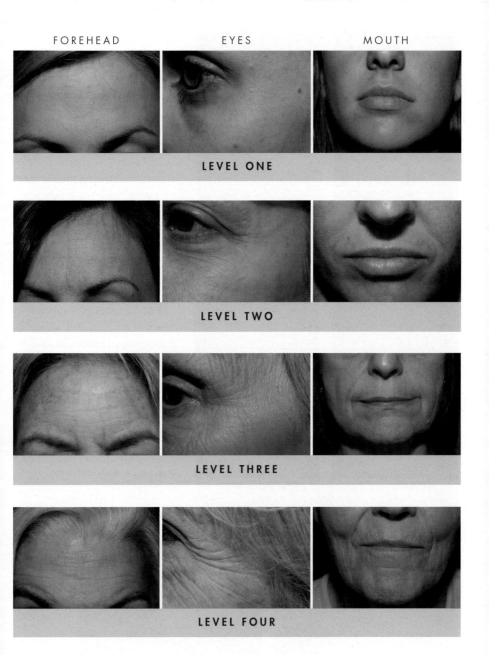

FOREHEAD EYES MOUTH

LEVEL ONE

LEVEL TWO

LEVEL THREE

LEVEL FOUR

As the aging levels increase, the depth and number of wrinkles increase for each of the areas shown, as does laxity.

Predicting How and Where You Will Age

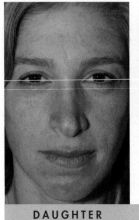
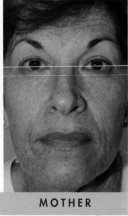

| DAUGHTER | MOTHER |

GENETICS: Note how the daughter is showing similar aging patterns as her mother, particularly around the mouth and eyes.

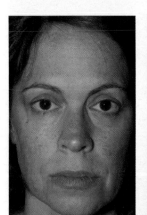
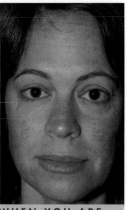

HOW YOU LOOK WHEN YOU ARE TIRED VS. WELL RESTED

SLEEP: The face as it appears when you are tired (*left*) shows future aging patterns that usually disappear when you've had enough sleep. Note the lines around the eyes, the increased skin laxity around the mouth, and the deepening of old acne scars on the cheeks. As you age, you may have these concerns even when you've had enough sleep.

THE CRINKLE BEFORE THE WRINKLE

PROGRESSION: Barely perceptible crinkling of the skin, often a result of sun damage, will progress to noticeable fine lines.

THE WEAR AND TEAR OF MOVEMENT: As we age, lines that appear when we make facial expressions will become permanent even when we are expressionless. Botox injections help prevent this progression.

WITHOUT EXPRESSION   **WITH EXPRESSION**

FOREHEAD

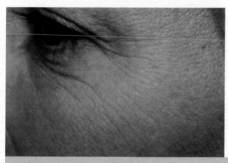 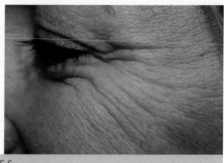

EYES

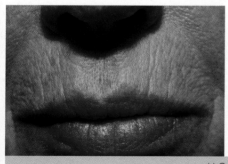 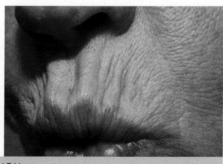

MOUTH

The Benefits from a Series of Alpha Beta Peels

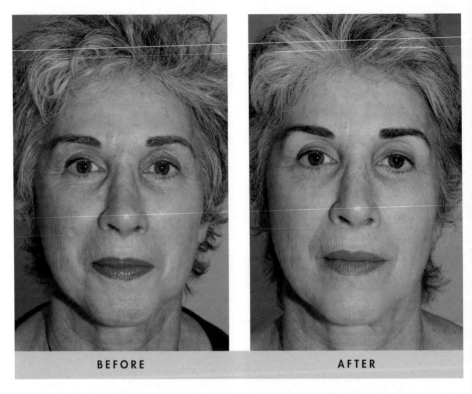

BEFORE   AFTER

This patient received four noninvasive peels performed monthly. Note the improvement in fine lines (eyes and cheeks), acne scars (cheeks), and overall skin tone.

The Benefits from a Series of Nonablative Laser Treatments

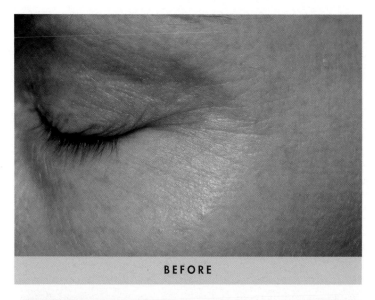

BEFORE

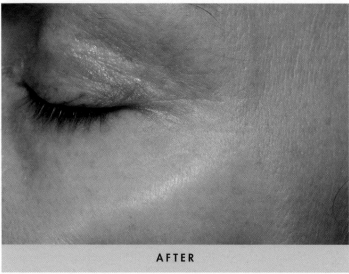

AFTER

This patient received six Smooth Beam laser treatments for her crow's feet. Her skin was mildly red for only twelve hours after each treatment.

The Benefits from One Session of Botox Treatments

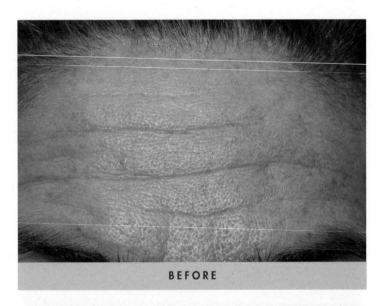

BEFORE

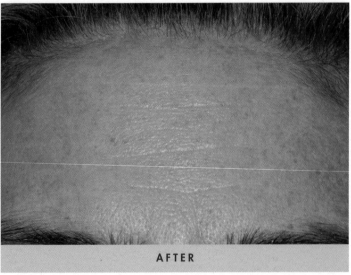

AFTER

Botox relaxes the skin and reduces lines on the forehead as shown, but also around the eyes and in between brows.

The Benefits from Using an Injectible Filler to Reduce Deep Lines and Folds

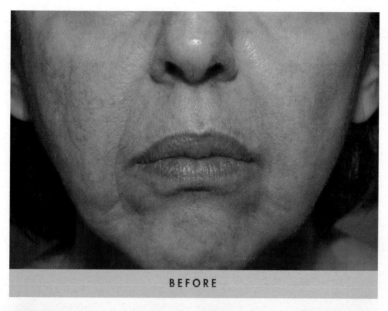

BEFORE

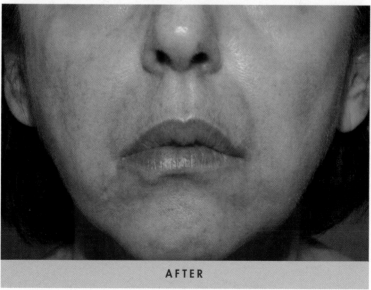

AFTER

The patient shows nearly full correction of the nasolabial folds after receiving two syringes of Restylane.

The Works

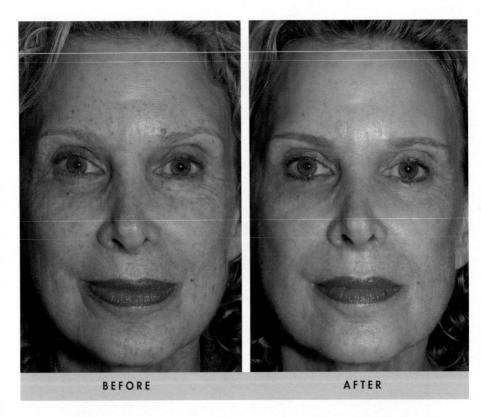

BEFORE

AFTER

This patient received a combination of treatments over three months: four in-office Alpha Beta peels, four Smooth Beam treatments around the eyes, Botox in the forehead, YAG laser for sunspots, Pulse-Dye laser for the red growths, Restylane into the nasolabial folds, and daily antiaging products.

in the next two chapters (Levels Three and Four) since they may be appropriate choices for your skin as it matures.

For now, we will limit our discussion to the temporary soft-tissue fillers, which are all injected beneath the skin's surface to add a youthful-looking fullness to under-eye hollows, wrinkles, the deep lines that run from the nose to the mouth, and sunken cheeks (see photo section, pages 7 and 8). The discomfort caused, the longevity of the results, and how long it takes to see the full benefits all vary with the substance being injected. While there is no significant downtime associated with any temporary soft-tissue filler, some short-lived bruising, swelling, and redness may occur afterward. Complications are extremely rare but may include infection. If you are pregnant, suffer from an autoimmune or a connective tissue disease such as lupus, you should contact your physician even before consulting a dermatologist.

Collagen

Until the introduction of the hyaluronic acid-based fillers Restylane, Perlane, and Hylaform, bovine collagen was considered to be the gold standard in filling. But even with younger and more glamorous, newer kids on the block winning rave reviews, collagen is still widely used and the preferred filler of many doctors and patients alike. Bovine collagen is a fibrous substance purified from cowhide turned into a liquid and then mixed with lidocaine, a local anesthetic. It is this addition of lidocaine that often makes collagen the most appealing option. While the injections can pinch, collagen is not as painful as any of the others—though any filler injected into the lips is painful because the lips are highly sensitive.

Because it is derived from cows, it is considered to be a foreign substance to the human body and can cause allergic reactions. To ensure you don't have one, around two months before your first treatment, your doctor should inject a tiny sample of collagen into your forearm (called a skin test). If redness, swelling, or itching occurs within three weeks, then you are not a good collagen candidate. If none of these symptoms occur, your doctor will do another test. If like most people you don't have any problems, then you'll get the green light.

There are two kinds collagen: Zyderm, which is thinner and injected less deeply and therefore lasts a short time, and Zyplast, which is thicker and injected more deeply and lasts somewhat longer. While it may seem like a no-brainer to opt for Zyplast over Zyderm to get more bang for your buck, Zyplast can look lumpy and uneven if used in finer crevices. At Level Two, you almost certainly will be more of a candidate for Zyderm since any indentations you may have are most likely fairly shallow, though Zyplast may be a more appropriate choice if you have deep creases in the nasolabial folds. As your face matures, you may want to consider using a combination of the two.

The biggest problem my patients have with collagen is that its longevity isn't all that impressive. In my experience, its average lifespan is about three months, and all too often it disappears in less time than that.

Hyaluronic Acid Fillers

Like collagen, there are different varieties of hyaluronic-acid-based fillers: Restylane and Hylaform for finer lines, and Perlane for deeper ones. All are perfectly replicated, synthesized hyaluronic acid, which, as discussed, occurs naturally in the skin as a means of first drawing and then trapping in water. Because hyaluronic acid is found in our bodies, you do not need to undergo a skin test for allergic reactions. I personally have gotten amazingly smooth, even, and natural-looking results from these fillers, and my patients have been equally happy. My colleagues also report similar results. Both Perlane and Restylane tend to last longer than either version of collagen. Depending on the person, results can be evident for up to six to twelve months. The one drawback is that neither one of them is formulated with any anesthetic so a topical numbing cream as well as injections of an anesthetic nerve block may be required. (**PLEASE NOTE:** At the time of this writing, Perlane is still pending FDA approval but has been widely used in Europe for years.)

Kerrie, a very tall and thin marathon runner, now forty, came to me in her midthirties, with deep creases in the nasolabial folds, which she said seemed to have appeared overnight. They were actually the result of her gaining and losing her pregnancy weight. Once her skin had lost some of its elasticity, the lines were so entrenched she might actually have been considered a good candidate for a face-lift, even at such a young age. Instead, we simply filled them in with Restylane, which plumped them back out to their former youthful state.

For Jennifer, who was in her midthirties, the only signs of premature aging that bothered her were the acne scars that seemed to deepen with age. But getting rid of them was the easiest thing in the world. We first did a few sessions with the Smooth Beam laser to smooth and soften them and then filled in any remaining depressions with Restylane. The once quite prominent scars are now virtually invisible.

Autologus (Your Own) Fat Transfer

This treatment actually consists of two procedures so I don't find it to be especially time or economically efficient, but it can work wonders on sunken eyes. During the first procedure, your doctor uses a cannula—a slim probing tube attached to a vacuum—to liposuction out a *little* bit of fat, usually from the buttocks, hips, or thighs. Who wouldn't like to lose a little fat where we don't want it? But the operative word here is *little*. We're talking 30 ccs or about 12 tablespoons of fat. If the doctor takes enough fat out that you will notice it, you run the risk of having a divot left in that area and are venturing into the realm of full-scale liposuction.

The tiny amount of fat is then cleansed with a saline solution and injected into your face under local anesthetic. One of its great benefits is that since the fat comes from your own body, you can't be allergic to it. But in my experience, I have found the results of fat injections to be variable. The fat can migrate into other areas of your face and so may not lie where you put it. It also generally requires at least two rounds of injections and, since so much of the fat injected into your face is absorbed by the body, it usually requires the doctor to inject much more of it than you actually need (called overcorrection) so you are left with unsightly bulges for approximately two weeks. The process is then repeated. After the overcorrection diminishes, results can last longer than those of collagen but they are extremely variable. Considering how invasive this procedure is, it may not be worth it to you.

Many doctors will offer to store extra harvested fat for you for up to six months. This practice is akin to tissue banking, and it is not one I recommend. Plus, the government frowns upon it. The reason? There is a slight but nonetheless dangerous risk of a mix-up in the storage facility and you may get someone else's fat injected into you, which can result in a reaction and even disease transmission. If fat injections are your filler of choice, while it may be inconvenient and more expensive, it is best to start fresh every time.

Laboratory-Grown Human Collagen

Recently, the FDA has approved two types of human collagen grown under laboratory conditions—CosmoPlast for deeper lines and CosmoDerm for shallow ones. Like bovine collagen, both are mixed with lidocaine to help numb the areas being treated. Unlike collagen, neither substance requires any allergy testing because the collagen used is similar to the collagen normally found in your skin. In my experience, these fillers typically have the same longevity as bovine collagen.

Whatever line smoother or wrinkle plumper you choose to fill in problem areas as a Level Two, it is important to keep in mind that you have an enormous opportunity to prevent further damage and reverse any damage that has already been sustained. The key, though, is to do nothing drastic or permanent that may not look good over time as your face ages and changes shape (for example, cheekbone implants, permanent fillers, or a face-lift). Your best course of action is to climb the ladder in terms of aggressiveness by exploring the noninvasive procedures and antiaging products that are geared to your specific areas of vulnerability before you do anything else. Knowing that no one procedure or product can take the place of a healthy lifestyle and good daily skin-care habits will also help keep your skin looking beautiful for years to come.

5
Level Three

AGE-ERASING OPTIONS

If you're at Level Three (a score of 47–58), like many patients I see, you may look at yourself in the mirror with the critical eyes of an adolescent. You see all the problems that need fixing rather than all the features that make you the lovely person you are. The fact is, however, at this phase of your skin's life cycle, its degenerative abilities are surpassing its regenerative ones. While this may be a sobering if not depressing thought, do not dwell on it. In terms of turning back the clock, we've never had more exciting and efficacious ways to do it. And contrary to what many of my Level Three patients—mostly people in their midforties to early sixties—think before they start seeing me, it's not all about plastic surgery and/or aggressively invasive procedures anymore. At one time, three of the top plastic surgeries—face-lifts, forehead lifts, and lower and upper eyelid surgeries (blepharoplasties)—may have been the most widely prescribed options for people who were bothered by sagging, deep creases, lines, and wrinkles. True, they are still the only means to dramatically tighten severely sagging skin, but today these surgeries are just part of a continually expanding menu of nonsurgical services available to us.

While according to the American Society of Plastic Surgeons (ASPS), Level Three comprises the majority of people who opt for plastic surgery, all of the above operations have become less popular across the board. The ASPS reports from years 2000 to 2003, the total number of face-lifts performed decreased 4 percent, brow lifts were down 52 percent, and blepharoplasties fell 25 percent. Meanwhile, the number of noninvasive Botox injections that were administered increased by 267 percent.

No doubt one of the major reasons for these declines is our increased knowledge of how to protect ourselves from the sun and free-radical damage. New topical ingredients also build collagen, which helps to make our skin younger looking than ever before across all age groups. The decline in surgery can also be attributed to the growing number of less invasive, less expensive, and more natural-looking alternatives that are now more widely available— be it Botox, injectible fillers, peels, or laser resurfacing.

A prime concern of my Level Three patients is that they feel like they look tired all the time, even when they are well rested. This is actually due to the fact that as we mature, there is an overall lengthening of the face. Our noses drop, the skin around the jaw descends, the fat pads in the cheeks and under-eyes fall, and gravity exerts a fiercer pull. But there is much you can do to counteract this downward slide without undergoing the knife. Still, don't get caught up trying to look like an airbrushed picture in a magazine. I can tell you firsthand that for the most part, the celebrities and models you see pictured in those glossy pages don't look like that way in real life. My advice to you is to focus on looking like a healthier, more vital version of *you*. And listen to your own instincts. You alone have to decide how you want to look, which issues bother you, and what you are willing to do to achieve your goals. Joan, fifty-two, for example, gets Botox to relax the lines in her forehead but leaves the ones around her eyes because both she and her boyfriend think they are sexy. Someone else might feel exactly the opposite way.

Despite social or cultural pressures, it is unwise to aim for perfection. You have to weigh the risks of complete correction versus leaving yourself with somewhat of a line or wrinkle so you don't look unnatural or create a new problem that can arise as a result of being too aggressive. Be organized and plan out with your doctor exactly which issues trouble you the most and how you'd like to tackle them. But don't do everything all at once. You might find that after you take care of one thing, such as relaxing the lines around your eyes, you aren't affected by any of the other things that seemed so disconcerting before. Very often, making little improvements such as removing brown spots, broken capillaries—even a mole—can make such a dramatic difference in your appearance that you won't feel the need to do anything else.

Now may not be a bad time to make more permanent adjustments with longer-lasting fillers, surgical implants, or even plastic surgery if you've been taking the less invasive measures already discussed and are still not happy with your appearance. If that idea appeals to you, you might first want to try the less invasive but somewhat more aggressive measures discussed in this chapter. If you are looking for still further changes, turn to chapter 6 (Level Four) to learn about more aggressive measures and about plastic surgery. We discuss the more permanent fillers in this chapter since they are still far less invasive than surgery of any kind. But again, take your time in making any decision and only go for established treatments and procedures. There are enough safe, wonderfully successful ways to erase the signs of aging that you never have to put yourself at risk with something that hasn't stood the test of time.

The Basics

If you're just starting out on your antiaging campaign, it's important to realize that no one ingredient or procedure can replace a good solid daily skin-care routine with a cleanser and moisturizer geared to your skin type, gentle daily exfoliation, plus products with proven active ingredients to increase skin-firming collagen production and protect your skin from free radical and sun damage. Below are some minor adjustments and a few simple additions to the daily skin-care plans outlined in chapters 3 and 4. These substitutions and inclusions, along with the other basic measures previously described, can make a significant difference in helping you both to achieve and maintain a beautiful, healthier complexion if you use them as the foundation of your skin-care regimen. They will also enhance and extend the benefits of any other treatment or procedure you may choose.

1. TAKE CARE OF YOURSELF

Eating well, sleeping enough, drinking sufficient amounts of water, and getting regular exercise may sound like clichéd advice but doing what we can to stay healthy is the single biggest beauty bonus of all. You may have already noticed that you just don't seem to bounce back as quickly as you used to from an illness, a sleepless night, or one that involved free-flowing champagne and dancing into the wee hours. As we age, our built-in reserves, which help us combat all types of stressors, become depleted. This makes routine aggressors like the sun, lack of sleep, or alcohol that much more taxing because we have fewer and less potent internal resources with which to combat them.

I am not, by the way, suggesting that you stop having any fun at all, totally cut out the foods you enjoy, give up wine, and chain yourself to the treadmill. If your overall lifestyle is healthy, skipping a workout, staying out late, and eating a porterhouse steak once in a while are fine. But your body will be better able to withstand your chosen occasional "vices" if you've been taking care of yourself all along. It's the cumulative results of our daily habits that have the most impact on our lives. To that end, getting regular checkups, complete with blood work, and being diligent about taking prescribed medication will protect your health and keep your skin looking its best. You will find more detailed health and nutrition advice in chapters 7 and 8.

2. ASSESS YOUR SKIN TYPE

If the cleanser that has always been perfect for you now leaves your face dry, tight, or irritated, or if you've started reacting to a product or ingredient that never bothered you before, you are not alone. As we age, our skin becomes drier, more easily dehydrated, and thinner, which can make it more reactive. Switching to a milder version for sensitive, dry, or even very dry skin may be the only substitution you have to make to remedy the situation. But if active ingredients continue to bother you, try taking the steps outlined in "Customizing Your Daily Regimen," pages 71–72. If you still are uncomfortable, you can trade down to the nonprescription counterpart of an ingredient such as retinol instead of Renova. And don't worry that you will no longer see results if you take a step back and proceed with caution. As discussed, avoiding irritation helps to prevent the free radicals that accelerate the aging process. Plus, even if they are somewhat less potent, you will still be using a multitude of active ingredients that are proven age beaters.

3. USE A MORE EMOLLIENT MOISTURIZER

Over time your skin's natural hyaluronic acid stores and water content diminish. In addition, your body's estrogen production, which is a key factor in keeping skin looking youthful, also starts to decline—notably over age forty—and your natural lipid supplies dwindle, which means your skin's ability to retain moisture is compromised further. But these are actually relatively easy problems to fix. If your skin is still dry after you change cleansers, switching to a heavier moisturizer at night is a surefire way to regain what time has taken away. If your face still isn't completely comfortable, use it in the morning, as well.

4. BALANCE YOUR HORMONES

It's been well documented that peri- or postmenopausal women notice many less-than-favorable changes to their skin. Concerns can range from deeper lines and wrinkles to rough patches and increased sagging. It has always been thought to be due to the body's decline in estrogen, but the scientific community wasn't 100 percent sure about the actual role estrogen played in keeping skin looking vital. Promising breakthrough research, however, may have solved this mystery and, hence, the problem. Scientists have recently discovered that the collagen-producing fibroblasts in skin cells have estrogen receptors, which means that estrogen plays a significant role in collagen synthesis. As estrogen production slows, you have less and less of the hormone to go to the receptors to stimulate collagen production.

A positive side effect of hormone replacement therapy (HRT), which was originally prescribed to prevent heart disease and osteoporosis in menopausal women and then shunned due to new research that showed it might play a role in breast cancer, was that it imparted a healthier-looking complexion. It increased the skin's water content and collagen production thus making it more supple, plump, moist, and firm. Patients who went off of HRT, due to the new health concerns, immediately noticed a difference in their skin's appearance.

Here, too, it is completely possible to jump-start what the body no longer produces or that it produces in limited quantities. Genistein, the ingredient we discussed in the "Bolster Your Natural Defenses" section, page 61, as a means of inhibiting the enzymes that destroy collagen, has been shown in favorable overseas research to work on estrogen receptors like actual estrogen when applied topically without any of the side effects of HRT. Studies have indicated that after three months of twice daily application, genistein can increase the thickness of skin by at least 10 percent. While 10 percent may not sound like all that much, biologically it is huge and so will create dramatic and visible results.

A diet that includes soy isoflavonoids has also been shown to alleviate some symptoms associated with menopause, including hot flashes and dry skin, as well as play a role in preventing heart disease and certain cancers. For more details on soy's health and skin-beautifying benefits, see pages 177–79 in chapter 8.

3. INTENSIFY THE FIGHT AGAINST FREE RADICALS

Because, as we age, we have fewer natural defenses against damaging free radicals, it is doubly important now to use products with combinations of antioxidants and to have adequate supplies of them in your diet to help protect and preserve your skin.

4. SOAK IN SULFUR SPRINGS

Since ancient times people have been drawn to sulfur springs, claiming a good long soak soothed their aches and pains and gave them more vibrant and healthy-looking skin. In recent years, sulfur, in the form of MSM and chondroitin sulfate, has been included in supplements designed to relieve the joint pain associated with certain types of arthritis. It is believed that sulfur plays a role in preventing the degeneration of the cartilage (connective tissue) between joints. The connective tissue in joints is similar to the connective tissue of skin, and indeed sulfur has also been found to be present in the amino acids that comprise collagen. Based on favorable holistic studies and research from Europe, I believe incorporating sulfur into skin-care products and into a healthy diet could have a huge impact on preventing the signs of aging. (See chapter 8 for more details on sulfur's nutritional value.) While this belief has not yet filtered into mainstream skin care, I am so convinced of its regenerative abilities that I have recently added MSM to several products in the M.D. Skincare line. MSM is also present in some creams currently sold in health food stores.

5. REMEMBER YOUR HANDS

As with their chest and neck areas, many of my Level Three patients feel that their hands look older than their faces. Unfortunately, hands often do have an accelerated aging process because they are literally skin on bone without any fat to plump them up. Your feet are the only part of the body with the same structure. The hands are also often neglected in terms of sunscreen application so, as we mature, the cumulative effects of a lifetime of sun damage can take their toll in the form of brown spots, crinkling, and rough, dry patches. But never underestimate your power to change things. Washing with a milder soap, applying sunscreen before going outside, and keeping your hands well moisturized can greatly improve their appearance today and prevent further damage tomorrow. For an even bigger boost, start treating them the same way you do your face, chest, and neck. Put your hands on a daily topical regimen of vitamin C, antioxidants, retinol, and exfoliating acids. Within months, you will see a huge difference. Incorporating at-home and/or in-office light peels, as directed, will give you even better results.

Food for Thought

Human Growth Factor: The Next Miracle Antiaging Ingredient?

A naturally occurring substance in skin, human growth factor (HGF) has been shown to be an important component in both skin-cell regeneration and collagen formation. Originally researched as a way to heal severe wounds and burns, scientists have been synthetically engineering the several different types of HGF in labs or harvesting them from skin. Recently, it has become an ingredient used in some antiaging skin-care products. There has been concern in the medical community, however, that since some types of human growth factor may induce an abnormal rate of cell regeneration, it could have negative effects on the body. There have been no long-term conclusive studies to figure out how human growth factor actually works; what happens when you give people more of it than they should have at a certain age; if it's safe; if it even works; and if so, which type and at what concentrations. Human growth factor in skin care is being further explored and it is also being closely watched. Stay tuned.

6. LEARN TO LOVE HUMIDITY

Dry climates, be it indoors or outdoors, literally suck the moisture out of skin. Humid climates impart it. Using humidifiers in
your house throughout the winter—when the air is driest due
to the cold and in-door heating systems—and in the summer
when you have the equally skin-parching air-conditioning on—
will help to keep moisture in your skin despite the dehydrating
conditions.

Food For Thought

Plumping Up Hands with Fillers

Recently, it has come into fashion to use fat injections to try to
fill out a bony, less-than-youthful-looking hand. While I don't
think this procedure will hurt you, since the fat is coming from
your own body, I don't know how much it can actually help. Remember, your hands naturally don't have any fat in them in the
first place so adding what was never there may look unnatural.
In addition, there have been few, if any, published studies on the
results or longevity of this procedure. Considering that fat injections require the two-step process of first harvesting fat from another part of your body and then injecting it elsewhere—not to
mention the necessity for overcorrection that can look unsightly
for weeks—and then a second round of injections, I think it's important that you speak to people who have had the procedure and
see the results firsthand rather than just looking at pictures in the
doctor's office. Before you make your final decision, speak to the
same people again three months later so you can really assess its
benefits and lifespan.

Specialized Treatment for Problem Areas

With many of my Level Three patients, making the above adjustments to their daily regimen, plus adding one or two of the procedures in Level Two: "Specialized Treatment for Problem Areas" pages 73–89) are all they need to be completely satisfied with their skin.

Hilary, fifty-three, felt like she looked tired all the time. Her deep lines around her eyes, lax upper lids, general crinkling, and sagging around the jowls were troubling to her. Objectively speaking, she could have been a realistic candidate for a face-lift or, at the very least, upper eyelid surgery (blepharoplasty). But she was dead set against elective cosmetic surgery of any kind and wouldn't even consider it a possibility. We did five sessions of full-face noninvasive Smooth Beam laser treatments, several in-office peels, and a little Botox on the forehead and around the eyes. She also started a daily skin-care regimen that included wearing sunscreen, using antioxidant products—specifically ones with vitamin C, plus P. emblica and MSM—and at-home peels. Now, her skin tone, texture, and firmness are greatly improved, the lines far less visible, and she has a newfound radiance. She is absolutely delighted with the results.

Roberta, fifty-five, was so unhappy with her drooping brow and lined forehead that she first consulted with a plastic surgeon, even before making an appointment with me. He recommended a brow lift operation. The surgeon also recommended that she get a face-lift at the same time as the forehead lift because if he pulled her forehead tight enough to make an appreciable difference, the rest of her face would look slack in comparison. In the end, she still might have needed Botox to stop the wear and tear that caused the lines in the first place. Very frightened of plastic surgery, especially what subjectively seemed to her to be two such radical operations, she made an appointment with me and we opted for a series of in-office peels, solid at-home skin care, and Botox in her forehead. We could only get a 75 to 80 percent improvement because if we used enough Botox to make her forehead 90 percent better, it would make her upper lids and brow, both of which had a tendency to sag, droop further. Nonetheless, the results were dramatic. She was and continues to be thrilled with the results of this game plan.

Sometimes, keeping a little extra weight on and preventative measures can make all the difference. Emily, fifty, was truly a genetic miracle. She came to me when she was forty-five, with no obvious need to tweak her regimen. She looked like she was in her thirties. Still, she wanted to prolong her youthful appearance. She started using the full spectrum of antiaging ingredients in at-home products as well as getting in-office peels once a month, plus doing a little Botox on the few faint lines of her forehead that were just making their presence known. At the same time, she made the conscious decision to stop trying to lose "those last five pounds" and actually gained weight to fill out her "fashionably" ultrathin frame and face. She still has a great figure, by the way. Her friends and husband were completely perplexed and not all that pleased that she was spending so much time and money trying to eradicate skin problems she clearly didn't have. Five years later, everyone is amazed at how fantastic she looks, especially in comparison to her peers. She truly could pass for thirty-five.

So if there are things about your face that you'd like to change, and you feel the need to kick it up a notch from the strategies outlined in the last chapter, you can try trading up to the strategies outlined below, which may simply be a matter of combining a few of the Level Two measures. If you still are less than thrilled, you might want to consider the more aggressive tactics described in chapter 6 (Level Four), where you will read about Virginia, fifty-two, extremely youthful looking in every way except for the prominent lines around her mouth, who opted to go all out with deep laser resurfacing.

RELAXING LINES AND PLUMPING UP WRINKLES:
BOTOX AND FILLERS

If you've already tried using Botox or a filler for specific regions of concern, you might be finding that using either one alone isn't offering you a satisfying enough correction. And if you're just starting out, your doctor may advise you to treat certain lines and wrinkles with a one-two punch of both injectibles. The reason? Lines that are the result of wear and tear from facial contractions may still be visible now when your face is no longer making an expression. Conversely, lines that are plumped up with soft-tissue fillers may no longer be visible when your face is at rest but appear when you are making an expression. If either one of these scenarios is the case, I recommend first treating the area with Botox to minimize the wear and tear that caused the line in the first place and then a filler to plump up any remaining depression. The depth of the line or crease will determine which type of filler will be the most effective. The thicker Perlane and Zyplast are perfect for deep creases, such as the nasolabial folds, entrenched wrinkles, and acne scars. Zyderm and Restylane are better for finer lines. Getting Botox before any filler will also increase its longevity since it won't be worn away as quickly by muscle contractions.

Sometimes a line can exist within a crease. If this is the case, first have it filled in with the thicker Perlane or Zyplast. Wait a week to see the effects, and then layer Restylane, Zyderm, or Cosmodem into the remaining line. Different areas of the face often require different filling, Botoxing, and other antiaging tactics. Here are some specifics.

The Nasolabial Folds

For the deep creases that run along the sides of the nose down to the mouth, soft tissue fillers are, for now, the best game in town unless you opt for a face-lift to pull them upward and outward (see photo section, page 7). However if you seek to completely eradicate those creases through plastic surgery, you may have to be pulled extremely tight, which can result in an unnatural look.

In terms of fillers, generally the thicker Perlane and Zyplast offer the most satisfactory results in this region. Medium to deep laser and peel resurfacing (see "Reducing the Appearance of Lines, Lightening Sunspots, Tightening Lax Skin, and Spurring Collagen Production in One Fell Swoop," pages 115–120, for more details on those treatments) cannot firm up severe sagging and can even be dangerous if either one is cranked up to the intensity where they could theoretically burn the skin. Permanent scars, burns, hyperpigmentation, and hypopigmentation are just a few of the side effects that could result. Botox is also not an appropriate treatment for this area.

Brow and Forehead

Botox is still the best option for easing lines in the forehead and the muscles between the brows, called the glabella, (see chapter 3, for specifics). Fillers may be used to some extent in the glabella. Forehead lines, on the other hand, have no anatomical valley to fill in, so only Botox works well there. (See photo section, page 6.) Fillers may be used in the glabella to some extent, but it can be a tricky business because it contains a complex network of blood vessels. If you inject too much filler too deeply, there is a rare but serious risk that it could temporarily cut off circulation to the area, which can cause ulcerations of the skin. Using a moderate amount of Zyderm and Restylane injected very superficially can plump up any loose, flaccid skin in the areas that look different from the rest of the forehead. You can get really good results with just a tiny amount. It is far better to keep a little bit of a line than to push the hand of your doctor to go deeper. A light hand is equally important when filling in bagginess in the glabella. You don't want to risk having it puff out over the bridge of the nose, which can create a Neanderthal effect. (See "Reducing the Appearance of Lines," pages 115–120 for all Botox specifics.)

Crow's-Feet

Peels, Renova, and nonablative laser treatments may not be enough to give you completely satisfying results now, but each one of them will still make a difference, especially when used in combination with one another. Botox to stop the wear and tear that causes the lines would be your next addition. When seeking to soften the lines around the eyes, it's important to make sure you don't completely immobilize the lines that appear when you smile or talk. Otherwise, you may compromise your ability to open your mouth normally. To treat this area safely and effectively, your doctor should inject three shots at the very corner of the outer eye 1/16 inch below the bone of the eye socket spanning no more than 1/2 inch vertically down to the top of the cheekbone. The three injections should be no more than 1/4 inch apart. While this precision may be a bit nitpicky, it is necessary to avoid complications. When Botox is injected too low in the face, it can disable the cheekbone muscles. When this occurs, your smile is greatly affected since your cheeks won't rise and your upper lip won't turn up at the corners when you smile. If you look at some young Hollywood starlets who suddenly seem to have peculiar looking smiles, it is most likely because they have had Botox injected improperly into this region or into the bunny lines (the lines or wrinkles on the sides of the nose that are exacerbated by facial contractions). If you have puffy under eyes as well as lines, talk to your doctor about placing the injections farther horizontally out to the ear. This way when you smile, your eyes will still stretch outward a bit so the puffiness will spread out rather than accumulate in a smaller area.

For more correction, you can try some nonablative laser treatments, done after the Botox injections so you can see the regions that require extra attention. Any remaining lines can be treated with the thinner Restylane or Cosmoderm after the laser treatments so the heat from the laser doesn't break either filler down. The thicker Perlane and Cosmoplast can create bumps and uneven results in this area since the skin under the eyes is especially thin. For a more aggressive laser procedure, see "Reducing the Appearance of Lines," pages 115–120.

The Lips

While many younger women want to make their lips plumper, thinning lips can become more of a major concern for my Level Three patients. Injectible fillers such as collagen, Perlane, and Restylane, can create believably attractive-looking fuller lips if you and your doctor are moderate in your expectations. The starlets with the overblown bee-stung pouts are typically going for this look to create a certain effect on camera. It doesn't necessarily translate into real life situations. Often, fat injections (see chapter 4, Level Two for more details) are recommended to plump up this area but, given that the treatment requires two procedures and two rounds of injections with overcorrection that leave you with unsightly bulges for approximately two weeks after each one, you might want to consider the easier-to-use and more efficient collagen or hyaluronic acid-derived fillers instead. In my experience, I also have found the results of fat injections to be variable because the fat can migrate into other areas of your face.

Lines above the upper lip can be especially troubling for women as they age because as they become deeper, lipstick can start to bleed into them. If nonablative laser treatments and light peels aren't giving you the results you want, you can trade up to medium-depth laser, resurfacing, or peels. Injecting fillers into these lip lines can also yield highly successful results, particularly if your doctor injects the filler into the perpendicular lines around the border of the lips. These lines are often neglected when the overall mouth is being treated because they are fairly faint in comparison to the others. But plumping them up (even if you don't get a filler administered anywhere else in the skin above the upper lip) will significantly rejuvenate this area. It will also help to prevent your lipstick from bleeding.

THE MORE PERMANENT PLUMPERS

If the idea of a lifetime of regular filler injections is less than appealing, it may be tempting to consider some of the more permanent fillers. For now, these include Radiance, Artecoll, and silicone. Permanent, however, is a relative term. While silicone has been proven throughout the years and in numerous clinical trials to be permanent, no long-term studies on the longevity of Radiance and Aretcoll are available since these substances haven't been used cosmetically for a long period of time. But since they are longer lasting than anything else out there and may require surgery to have them removed, it is paramount that you select a doctor who is highly skilled in administering any of the above-mentioned fillers. So far, studies have shown that these more permanent fillers are good in deeper grooves, such as crater-like acne scars and the nasolabial folds. It is very hard to get good results for lip lines and lip plumping, crow's-feet, and lines in the forehead. While I have seen some good results with these more permanent plumpers, horror stories in medical journals abound. So proceed with caution.

In addition to speaking to as many people as you can who've had any of these treatments, I also recommend that if you decide to go for it, only correct a little bit at a time; then wait for six weeks, see the results, and gradually add more if need be. Never aim for full correction in one sitting. It may be more expensive and time consuming than having it all done at once, but it is one way to ensure that you will be happier with the results. Another way to make sure that you are the rule rather than the exception is to hedge your bets and go the conservative route. Ask your doctor to "permanently" fix only 80 percent of a concern rather than the whole nine yards. You can always supplement the results with temporary filler.

None of these permanent fillers are so far approved by the FDA for cosmetic use, but silicone and Radiance are FDA approved for other medical purposes. So if you choose to go the more permanent route, at least there are reputable, legitimate suppliers of those two substances that have to adhere to rigorous testing standards.

Liquid Silicone Microdroplets

Once only associated with breast implants that were potential health risks, silicone has recently been FDA-approved for ophthalmologic use (Aldatosil) and is currently being considered for reinstatement as a material for breast implants, as long as the manufacturers take the necessary steps to prevent the implants from leaking into the body. Silicone's true plumping benefits come from spurring collagen formation in much the same way a grain of sand sparks an oyster to create a pearl. Once silicone is injected, the body encapsulates each microdroplet with its own collagen, forming a tiny skin-plumping scar around the particle. The biggest problem with liquid silicone microdroplets as a cosmetic filler is that sometimes excessively large-volume shots are incorrectly injected, resulting in severe overcorrection, migration, and inflammation. Worse still, large sometimes painful, nodules occur, which very often can't even be surgically removed. A doctor who administers silicone microdroplets must be skilled in the art of undercorrection and be able to gauge how much silicone is needed to produce an appropriate collagen response to fill in a given area. The results are permanent.

Radiance

Made from calcium hydroxyl apatite, a natural component of bone and teeth, that has been synthesized into injectable microscopic spheres, Radiance has been FDA approved for use in the larynx and has been used in Europe for the past few years to plump up lines and scars, fill in nasolabial folds, and for lip enlargement. Initial studies indicate that Radiance appears to have little or no risk of allergy when used cosmetically and may last as long as five to seven years.

While you will see an improvement immediately after the procedure from the injection of the material itself, Radiance's microspheres spur collagen production in that region in much the same way as silicone microdroplets do—so it might take a few months for you to realize its full benefits. As with silicone, a doctor who uses Radiance must undercorrect and judge how much Radiance is needed to spur the right amount of collagen growth to plump up a given region. Otherwise, the results can look overblown and unnatural. Studies suggest that the microspheres disappear over the years, leaving your collagen as a semipermanent effect. Touch-ups may be required. Specific FDA approval for cosmetic use is expected in the near future.

Artecoll

This consists of a mixture of plastic microspheres, bovine collagen, and the anesthetic lidocaine. The collagen gives you more of an instant-gratification effect and then dissipates after a few months. The plastic microspheres remain indefinitely, prompting the body to produce collagen and scar tissue around them. While I have seen some good results when used in depressed scars and deep creases, there is a high incidence of bumpiness when Artecoll is used for lip augmentation. Again, the key to getting successful results is to undercorrect to allow for the skin's natural collagen formation to fill in an area rather than the Artecoll itself. Unfortunately, if you have any problems with it, the sphere has to be surgically removed, which could result in scarring.

UNDER-EYE BAGS AND DARKNESS

Other than the treatments outlined in chapters 3 and 4, and a blepharoplasty (surgically removing the vascular fat pads under the eyes that can erase darkness as well as deflate puffiness), these issues are pretty tough to tackle. As discussed, light peels, nonablative laser treatments, Renova, genistein, and vitamin C all can help to thicken skin so that the fat pads and any fluid accumulation have less of an opportunity to push skin outward. If you are only recently troubled by under-eye bags, and you are not genetically predisposed to them, you might want to talk to your doctor about having your thyroid tested.

Medium laser resurfacing with an Erbium laser can tighten skin, erase crow's-feet, *and,* to a lesser extent, lighten under-eye skin.

GENERAL SAGGING

Unfortunately, other than a face-lift, there are few options for firming up sagging skin, since fillers aren't appropriate for this problem. The less aggressive radio-frequency face-lift might eventually deliver the tightening results we've all been hoping for; but for now, building collagen through light peels, vitamin C, retinol, sulfur, and genistein while protecting your skin from the sun and free radicals with sunscreen and antioxidants is your best bet and still can deliver considerable improvement. I've also had some success with treating overall slackness with several noninvasive Smooth Beam full-face treatments and with the medium-depth Erbium laser.

Food for Thought

The So-Called Knifeless Face-Lifts: Too Good to Be True?

Electrostimulation: While this treatment has been a mainstay of spas and dermatologists' offices for several years, it frequently enjoys a resurgence in popularity. These days, it's being billed as an alternative to Botox. Little electrodes are placed on your face and then a low level current is turned on to stimulate muscle contraction. (Botox, on the other hand, stops it.) The idea behind this treatment is that if you can stimulate a muscle contraction maximally, it will stay that way, which will pull the skin up like a face-lift. Sort of like if you build a muscle through weight lifting, it will pull the skin tighter since it has to stretch to fit around it.

This logic might hold somewhat true for stimulating the muscles in the cheeks because you are contracting them in the same direction that a face-lift would pull up excess skin in the nasolabial folds. Results, however, in the best-case scenario, have so far been proven to last only a very brief time. Some studies report a beneficial lift of the eyebrow. The forehead, on the other hand, is an entirely different matter. Electrostimulation actually contracts the muscles in the same way that we wrinkle our foreheads, raise our eyebrows, and scowl. Making those facial expressions is what leads to the wear and tear that causes the lines in the first place.

Why artificially induce more of them? While some maintain that facial exercises work in much the same way as electrostimulation, I have never seen them work on any of my patients, nor have I seen any research proving their effectiveness.

The radio-frequency face-lift Known by the trade names Therma-Cool and sometimes Thermage, this treatment uses a handheld instrument to transmit an electric radio frequency through the skin to heat the collagen fibers below the surface causing them to contract and tighten, without burning the top layers. The premise is that radio frequency can heat the skin at higher temperatures than lasers can without burning the skin so it has more of a tightening effect than they do. Studies presented to the American Society for Laser Medicine and Surgery (ASLMS) have cited 25 to 50 percent improvements in tightening mild to moderate laxity in the nasolabial folds, forehead, the skin surrounding the eyes, and jowls. So it could quite possibly be "the next big thing."

But while the radio-frequency face-lift is garnering some buzz for being a breeze of a procedure, it isn't exactly painless. While the pulses of energy are being delivered, a cryogen cooling spray is simultaneously administered to help keep the surface of the skin from burning and minimize discomfort. But more anesthetizing is generally required. A topical numbing cream is also applied and local anesthetic injections administered. Some doctors are now also giving patients Percocet, intravenous sedation, or nerve blocks to help them manage what some anecdotal reports cite as intense pain. Reports on the downtime vary from no redness or discomfort at all to a week or more. So for now, it is difficult to gauge how long it will really keep you out of commission.

ThermaCool is FDA approved for treating laxity in the upper third of the face, with approval pending for the lower portion. While some doctors are raving about the results, the procedure is still in its infancy. Follow-up information on patients who have had it is based on only a few years, so potential long-term complications may not have had the chance to surface. In addition, the longevity of its results hasn't been established. It is also worth noting that so far it has only been shown to be beneficial in treating mild to moderate signs of aging and is not a substitute for a traditional face-lift. CO_2 and Erbium laser resurfacing are still recommended to treat more deeply wrinkled, sun-damaged skin.

If you do decide this is the procedure for you, again, I suggest you talk to as many people as possible who have had it so you can get an accurate picture of what it entails, what the end benefits are, and what the healing process is like. Before-and-after photos may show exciting results but they don't reveal the full picture. Time may prove radio frequency to be a valuable addition to the antiaging arsenal, particularly if the treatment is fine-tuned so it is less painful and improves more dramatic sagging. I, for one, am going to wait it out.

Coblation Short for *cold ablation,* this procedure, like radio frequency, uses a microelectrical radio frequency. But rather than spurring collagen production through heat stimulation to the fibroblasts, it actually disintegrates surface-damaged skin, like medium and deep laser and peel resurfacing. The formation of new collagen is the result of the skin's healing from this injury. I have only seen soft data based on poor clinical trials claiming Coblation's safety, effectiveness, and longevity. I have also treated two patients for scarring and burns as a result of this procedure. In addition, while the pain and downtime have been likened to that of nonablative procedures, anecdotal reports cite it to be far more like those of deep resurfacing treatments. As with the radio-frequency face-lift, this procedure is still in its infancy so follow-up information on patients who have had it is based on only a few years. Potential long-term complications may not have had the chance to surface. In addition, the longevity of its results hasn't been established. If you are considering coblation as an option, I would urge you to do your homework and speak to as many patients who have had it as possible before you make your decision.

Reducing the Appearance of Lines, Lightening Sunspots, Tightening Lax Skin, and Spurring Collagen Production in One Fell Swoop

If you've already tried the full spectrum of nonablative lasers and light acid peels and are still not completely satisfied with your skin's overall appearance, it might be time to consider resurfacing with a medium laser or peel. Unlike their lighter counterparts, which spur collagen production either by direct stimulation to the fibroblasts (laser) or from the chemical fluctuation of the skin as it goes from acidic to neutral (peels), medium peels and laser resurfacing actually disintegrate the damaged skin to "remove" wrinkles, discolorations, age spots, and crinkling. This controlled injury causes new collagen to form as the skin heals, making a face look smoother and more youthful as a result. They both also have somewhat of a tightening effect. And while you still may need Botox for remaining lines, and soft-tissue fillers in deeper indentations, medium resurfacing is an efficient and long-lasting way to treat several different issues simultaneously. Typically these treatments are performed only once every five to ten years as needed, but if you have a lot of sun damage, your doctor might recommend two treatments done in relatively quick succession. Deeper laser and peels should be performed before you receive any soft-tissue fillers or Botox.

The degree of improvement depends on the strength of the

peel or laser, the depth they penetrate, and the extent of the damage before treatment. But going all out can have its downsides—
the higher the heat of the laser or the strength of the acid, the
greater the risks, which might include scarring, hyperpigmentation,
and hypopigmentation, especially around the eyes and above the
upper lip. Medium, dark, and olive-toned skins are especially
prone to hypopigmentation and hyperpigmentation—the darker
the complexion, the greater these risks. Sometimes, both side effects can occur even if the peel or laser treatment is relatively
moderate. There really is no way to darken the areas that have become hypopigmented, though sometimes you can successfully
bleach the hyperpigmented ones. All too often, the aftermath of
overzealous resurfacing, particularly in places that have been overlapped (where the chemical solution or laser has passed over more
than once), is permanent, may not be concealable with makeup,
and looks worse than the original lines. It is important to discuss
these risks with your doctor and to proceed with caution and undercorrect, rather than trying to completely wipe out every last
problem and push the odds.

But enough of doom and gloom. If done right, medium-
strength peels and lasers offer tremendous overall benefits. The
trade-off for these benefits is that, unlike their noninvasive counterparts discussed previously, these procedures do require a recovery time.

For a medium peel, your doctor will most likely swab on a
mixture of trichloroacetic acid followed by a neutralizing solution. Medium laser resurfacing uses a carbon dioxide (CO_2) laser
turned down lower than for deeper projects. I personally prefer the
somewhat less aggressive Erbium laser. Both procedures are performed under local anesthetic through topical cream and injections. You may be given a prescription for an antibiotic and
antiviral medication to help prevent infection and possibly corti-

sone to help prevent swelling. Your doctor will advise you when and for how long you should take them.

While recovery time varies with skin type, your own natural healing abilities, and the depth of the procedure, skin typically remains oozy, swollen, and weepy for three to five days. Your skin can stay red to pink, which can be covered up with makeup, for an additional two weeks. I recommend you wait till any redness completely recedes before using any products other than a gentle cleanser, sunscreen, and a fragrance-free moisturizer. It is also critically important to avoid sun exposure, which can cause hyper-pigmentation in recently peeled or lasered skin and to wear at least an SPF 30 when you are outside.

Mona, fifty-six, felt that small, gradual changes from at-home products and light peels just wouldn't give her the more dramatic change she was looking for. A CEO at a major company, she felt that she needed to stay young looking to hold her own in the highly competitive business environment. She was not a candidate for a face-lift. About eight to ten pounds overweight, her face was relatively plump and firm—she simply didn't have enough excess skin to pull back. If she had that little bit "lifted," her face would have looked unnaturally "tight." We opted to do full-face Erbium laser resurfacing to give her a jump-start, so to speak. She got great results. Her skin was less lined, more even, radiant, and even firmer. She's been maintaining these results, which made her completely happy, for the last several years with in-office peels, daily home Alpha-Beta peels, and other products containing the key antiaging ingredients.

REGIONAL RESURFACING

Sometimes, it is possible to treat just one particular area, such as lines on the upper lip, if a full-face procedure isn't necessary. At this level, working regionally can be highly effective. As you mature, however, limiting treatment to just one area may make it look out of sync with the rest of the face. I also don't recommend regional treatments for people with medium to dark skin tones as there could be a marked change in skin pigmentation between the treated and nontreated areas.

CHOOSING BETWEEN THE TWO

Since medium and deep peels and laser resurfacing have the same risks and downtime, it may be difficult to decide which treatment to go for. I personally favor medium and deep laser resurfacing over medium and deep peels. I find that the laser offers more versatility. For example, you can turn it up a bit higher to treat more damaged areas and then gradually taper it back down for the rest of the face. A peel works uniformly so your only option is to rub it on harder in some places than in others, which can increase your risk of scarring, hypopigmentation, and uneven results. But your doctor can help you decide your best personal plan of action. In either case, it is important to make sure your doctor is highly skilled with a lot of experience in the procedure you choose. Neither method can cure sagging, including under-eye bags, because if the laser is turned up too high or the peel is too acidic, there is a huge risk of burning and scarring.

THE NECK, CHEST, AND HANDS—ESPECIALLY TRICKY AREAS

In my experience, the downsides of aggressively treating lines and wrinkles on these parts of the body far outweigh the benefits. The skin there, especially prone to mottling, brown spots, and broken capillaries from sun damage, is also very susceptive to the scarring, hyperpigmentation, and hypopigmentation that can be caused by medium to deep peels and laser resurfacing. I have also found that treating them with nonablative collagen-stimulating lasers doesn't really do all that much. The good news is that you can remove most of the obvious imperfections, which will make these areas look more youthful and healthy. While it may be impossible to completely turn back the clock in these regions, modern science is making strides every day. Promising wrinkle-treating lasers for the neck and chest are in development. Still, most of my patients find that just by conquering the most visible issues, they become completely satisfied with the appearance of their neck, chest, and hands and are no longer troubled by any remaining imperfections.

A YAG laser can wipe out the sunspots on the chest, arms, back, and hands. Broken capillaries can be zapped with a diode laser. Those red specks, called hemangiomas, that appear on the chest can be burnt off with an electrocauterization, which literally takes two seconds, causes little to no discomfort, and has no downtime except for tiny scabs, which fall off within days. In addition, at-home, spa, and in-office light acid peels can provide improvement in texture, clarity, and firmness in all of these regions but requires *several months* of treatment. Visible veins that aren't functional may be rendered less visible by two to three sessions of sclerotherapy—a saline solution is injected into the veins to collapse them. Tinier ones can be vaporized by a few sessions with a laser.

The neck is especially prone to sagging and deep lines as a result of genetics, dramatic weight loss, or sun damage. In terms of lines, it can have both vertical and horizontal ones. The vertical ones occur as the result of wear and tear from muscle contractions and so can be eased by Botox injections. The horizontal ones, on the other hand, are the result of sun damage and genetics and so are not good candidates for Botox.

The only thing that can truly help severe sagging there is a neck lift by a plastic surgeon. But proceed with caution as they are not always permanent and can offer varying results. Botox can provide a satisfactory but temporary alternative. It can relax the cords or bands that protrude from the neck that tend to sag with age and pull the neck downward. Once they are eased, unopposed upward muscular movement raises the neck, giving it the appearance of it being somewhat lifted.

Renee, fifty-seven, is a very thin woman with extremely thin skin. While her very high, prominent cheekbones could somewhat support the skin in her face to prevent it from sagging dramatically, there was no such structure in her neck. She was so bothered by her neck that she kept her blouses buttoned up to the very top button and began to favor turtlenecks. She was considering a neck lift but in order to achieve the most natural looking, symmetrical results, she was advised that she would also need a full face-lift or her neck would look completely out of sync with the rest of her face. Instead, we did several Botox injections in the neck, and it gave her enough of an improvement that she is now wearing scoop and V-neck tops.

Don't Underestimate the Power of Small Changes

Sometimes, the most minor adjustments can have a major impact. Ann, fifty-eight, was really bothered, and I mean *really* bothered, by the lines on the skin above her upper lip. We took the least invasive route first and treated them with several sessions of the Smooth Beam nonablative laser, which gave her a moderate improvement. She still wasn't 100 percent happy so we used Restylane to plump up any remaining indentations, which gave her even better results. However she was really aiming for perfection, which can be risky. I didn't want to get more aggressive with deep peels or laser since there was a good chance that either treatment would cause hypopigmentation, which would have looked worse than the lines. She found the answer herself and just got her teeth whitened. Low and behold, she has the most gorgeous smile. Now when you see her, you never notice any lines around her upper lip—not only have the lines been significantly reduced but she's also flashing this dazzling smile with her beautiful pearly teeth.

Imperfections can be rendered virtually invisible if there is something else wonderful about you. We know it to be the case for the personalities of the people we love. And the same holds true for the way you and other people perceive your appearance. Here, little alterations that can make a big difference:

* **Be Colorful:** Wearing color—any color—instead of black, white, or beige near your face can make you look like you've been getting eight to ten hours of sleep every night. If your style is shifted strictly into neutral, try wearing a bright scarf or colorful necklace.

* **Change Your Hairstyle:** Wearing long bangs, sweeping your hair to one side versus wearing a center part, and trimming it to shoulder length can all give the illusion of a fuller, i.e., younger-looking, face. Adding a *little* volume rather than blow drying it straight can also make you look more energetic.

* **Play with Your Hair Color:** Traditionally, the beauty industry has counseled women to lighten up their hair color as they get older. Going a shade or two lighter, or adding highlights around your face definitely can liven up the complexion. Going too light, however, can have the opposite effect. One of the things that gives the face luminosity is contrast, as in the contrast between your skin and hair color. If your hair is virtually the same color as your face, you will no longer have any complexion-brightening contrast.

* **Experiment with Makeup Shades:** Dark, super bright, and very pale pastel shades can make anyone look tired. Soft hues with some depth to them such as plums, chocolates, medium charcoals, rose, and medium pinks, on the other hand, will make you look more vital. If you are a die-hard red lipstick fan, adding more depth to it while downplaying some of its harshness by applying a light brown lipstick on top can make all the difference. The same goes for fuchsia and orange.

* **Brighten Your Smile:** In addition to bleaching your teeth, wearing a blue-based (cool-toned) lipstick can make your teeth look whiter and the whole face look younger and more vibrant as a result. Yellow-based lipsticks (orange, coral, peach, etc.) can have the opposite effect.

* **Wear Less Makeup:** Too much foundation and powder can settle into lines, creases, and pores, calling more attention to them, rather than cam-

ouflaging them. This can happen, by the way, to women of all ages. Layers of makeup can also make skin look overly matte, which definitely can suck the life right out of it. Try spot concealing over the places that need a little extra attention rather than wearing a full face of foundation.

* **Think Dewy:** Moisturizing and creamy formulations with a very subtle shimmer can make for a smoother makeup application while giving skin that "lit from within glow." Matte formulations are drying, plus they not only fail to impart light, but they also can rob you of it. Super shiny products with a white pearly opalescence can have the same effect.

* **Soften Your Eyebrows:** Super thin eyebrows can look severe and age the face. Somewhat fuller ones can erase years. If you don't have the patience to grow them back in, or find that years of plucking have stunted their growth cycle, use feathery strokes of a pencil one shade *lighter* than your hair color to fill them in a little bit. Bushy brows aren't the goal since they can also be aging; aim for softly full eyebrows.

Small cosmetic changes can all do wonders in terms of revitalizing your appearance and your self-confidence. So can embarking on a sound daily regimen that includes proven preventative and age-reducing measures, such as wearing sunscreen, using antioxidant products to guard against free radicals, acids to exfoliate, and vitamin C and/or retinol to spur collagen production. All these measures can still greatly improve the condition of your skin. When considering doing any of the more aggressive therapies we have already discussed, it is important not to let the media or your peers push you into making a rash, rather than a logical, decision. And once you have decided what improvements you wish to make, be organized and plan out your strategy rather than just randomly jumping into a procedure or product. Doing one thing at a time, rather than all at once, is also key. Fixing one problem, such as easing the furrow between your brows, may be all it takes to give you the results you were looking for. Plus, very often making little improvements such as removing brown spots or broken capillaries can make a dramatic difference in making you look more youthful.

My most important advice to you, especially at Level Three, is while it may be tempting to jump right into a new so-called miracle cure, don't buy into unproven hype. Go for what is tried and tested with proven results. Never put yourself in the position of being a guinea pig; your health and your face could suffer major consequences as a result. Besides, with so many safe and effective antiaging options out there, you can achieve a younger-looking, smoother, and more vibrant complexion without any risks at all.

6
Level Four

MAJOR CHANGES . . . OR NOT

Many women who are entering their sixties or seventies, at Level Four (a score of 59+) are feeling very positively about their looks and their lives. They have so much more self-confidence than they've ever had before—be it from life experience, successes at work, raising children, etc. In addition, they now feel more energetic and vital since their families have grown up, their careers are winding down, and they have more free time than they've had in years. Generally, they are happy with and are less focused on their appearance. They've made peace with the aging process of their skin and so don't have the desire to undergo anything drastic or invasive—especially if they or someone close to them has had to have any kind of a medical procedure. Perhaps this explains why Diana, a sixty-seven-year-old grandmother, scored a Level Two on the Life Cycle Quiz compared with her daughter, twenty-five years younger, who scored a Level Three.

Irene, sixty-eight, for example, made an appointment with me only because she was feeling pressured to "do something" to her face because a lot of her peers were getting plastic surgery. Up until that point she had been happy with her appearance. But now, all of a sudden, she was feeling insecure in comparison to her friends. But she also honestly felt they looked unnatural and was not an advocate of elective cosmetic surgery in the first place. We got her on a Level Two regimen of at-home peels, sunscreen, and vitamin C–based products, which all levels should be using daily. After several months, she was delighted with the results. She may not look as "young" as some of her friends, but she looks healthier and refreshed—a more vital version of herself, which was everything she had hoped for.

Many of my Level Four patients also have completely revised their priorities saying things to me like, "My cataract surgery lets me see now better than ever and I'm just so happy to be able to read and see clearly again. What do I care if there are lines around my eyes?"

On the other hand, some of my Level Four patients, especially those out in the workforce in competitive fields, feel like they want a more dramatic change, in order "to compete better" or simply to "look as young and energetic as they feel." Alicia, sixty-two, is an example. Not completely happy with her appearance, she came to me ready to make some changes. We worked her way up the ladder in terms of aggressiveness—lasered off brown spots and broken capillaries, used Botox in the lines around her eyes, Restylane in the ones above her lips, and put her on a routine of monthly peels to improve her skin's overall texture and firmness—but she still felt that she wanted to look better. So she got a full face-lift. Her surgeon was terrific and made her look completely natural—not forty—but a fresher, revitalized version of herself. She is delighted. Employed in the highly competitive investment banking industry, she says that she no longer worries that if she loses her job, no one else will hire her. This thought inspires her with a new self-confidence that actually radiates out of her.

But no matter how you perceive your appearance, or the actual condition of your skin, your options abound if you would like to make some kind of a change. You can still get good results from taking on the positive basic skin-care habits we outlined in chapters 3, 4 and 5 (Levels One, Two, and Three), as Irene did. If you desire more of a change, you can supplement the basics with in-office procedures such as peels, laser resurfacing, Botox, and fillers. Or you can make the decision to get some form of cosmetic surgery. The most important and gratifying thing to remember is that *any* change you make now will clearly be seen and impart you with more beautiful and healthy-looking skin. Even a moderate improvement in something that truly bothers you may have a huge impact in your appearance.

For this reason, I recommend to everyone at Level Four (who hasn't already) start with the least aggressive strategies and gradually work your way up to more intensive ones—only if *you* want to. While it may be difficult during these times of airbrushed perfection, it is important that you decide for yourself what you want and what you are willing to do to achieve it. Do not hold yourself up to standards that don't even exist in reality. It is also important that you don't let yourself feel pressured by friends or the news media to dive in all at once and dramatically alter your appearance if you are happy with it, or are on the fence about it, or looking to make a significant change. Remember, it is *your* face.

Martha, sixty-four, for example, was completely happy with the results she was getting from fillers, Botox, and peels until she came into contact with one too many face-lifted acquaintances. While she didn't want to undergo the surgery, she somehow couldn't help feeling that her appearance didn't measure up to these other women. After having a long heart-to-heart, we discovered that it was her hands, not her face, that were making her think she looked too old. So we lasered off the brown spots, which made her hands look at least a decade younger. Now, she is much more content with her appearance and is no longer considering plastic surgery.

If you don't want to deal with frequent injections and/or peels, or if your main concern is sagging skin, in the end, it could be more time- and cost-effective to have some cosmetic surgery—especially if you want a dramatic change and are not satisfied by the results of the less invasive procedures. It is worth noting, however, that while cosmetic surgery does reset the clock in terms of the way your skin looks, it doesn't resurrect the collagen-building machine, shield you from free radicals or the sun, or exfoliate the dulling dead skin cells that can still accumulate. So good daily skin-care habits will still be important. For this reason, women who've gotten face-lifts in their fifties, often get a second one in their sixties. You also may still decide to get Botox to minimize the lines caused by wear and tear or injectable fillers to plump up any remaining creases, which the face-lift failed to completely eradicate.

Should you decide to get plastic surgery, it is of paramount importance that you find a surgeon who has the proper qualification and is highly skilled and experienced in performing your procedure of choice. This may sound like a given, but the fact is that anyone with a medical degree can legally practice plastic surgery in the United States. In other words, you don't have to be a plastic surgeon to perform a face-lift. Your doctor should be board certified by the American Board of Plastic Surgery. Being a member of a surgical society, such as the American Society for Aesthetic Plastic Surgery (ASAPS) and/or the American Society of Plastic Surgeons (ASPS) indicates further qualifications and is proof that your doctor is board certified since both organizations only accept doctors who are. There are some organizations and societies, however, where doctors without the appropriate experience and training can buy their membership cerificates. I recommend that you check out any doctor you are considering with the American Board of Plastic Surgery. In addition, your anesthesiologist should be board certified by the American Board of Anesthesiology (ABA).

To make sure you and your surgeon are on the same page, it's a good idea to not only have several conversations with him about the look you want but also to speak with, and preferably see, some of the patients who have had aesthetic surgery performed by him. Before-and-after photos can be compelling, but they are only part of the picture. Your doctor should also be completely fluent in advanced and less invasive procedures such as endoscopic surgery, the minilift, and the subconjunctival blepharoplasty.

While some plastic surgeries and surgeons yield excellent results (Alicia, for example), I've seen too many patients who have face-lifts where they have been pulled so tight they look like they are walking through wind tunnels. They may look younger but they don't look like themselves anymore. If your priority is to look natural, you might discuss with your surgeon about going the moderate route (being pulled less tight) to preserve the natural architecture of your face. You can then plump up any remaining wrinkles with an injectible filler and use Botox to stop wear and tear. If you'd rather not be bothered by maintenance injections and want to look as young as possible, you may decide to go for an extreme face-lift. The point is, you have several choices in the type of surgery performed and the end result you want.

Never before have there been so many ways to turn back the hands of time. While it may make it more difficult for us to decide which methods are appropriate for us, these new technologies are bringing us closer than ever to looking vibrant and healthy at every stage in our lives.

The Basics

Here's how to adjust the daily skin-care plans outlined in chapters 3, 4, and 5 to better suit your specific needs. These additions and substitutions will help you to more precisely tailor your regimen and lifestyle habits to put you on the path to a gorgeous, radiant complexion. They will also enhance and extend the benefits of any other treatment or procedure you may choose to do.

1. TAKE CARE OF YOURSELF

Not to be an alarmist, but I personally think that it's a good idea to get a physical twice a year instead of just once when you are in your midfifties and beyond. The same goes for having your moles and general skin health checked by a dermatologist. Of course, if you are in overall good health and your physicians don't advise it, then it's probably not necessary. I do strongly believe, however, that it is important to treat any problem as it arises rather than waiting for it to become more serious. You know your body best. If you think there is something going on with you that merits a visit to your doctor, it most likely does. Making sure we are at the top of our game is truly the most powerful weapon we have in our antiaging arsenal. Taking prescription medications as directed, getting enough sleep, exercising regularly, and eating well are even more important now than they were just a few years ago. As we mature, our bodies' reserves continue to diminish, making it even more difficult to fend off and bounce back from stresses like the sun, alcohol, a high-fat diet, smoking, and lack of sleep. Anything you do to protect your health not only can have profound effects on your well-being but also on your appearance.

Blanche, seventy-two, for example had always been substantially overweight. Not happy with her appearance, she talked about getting a face-lift for years. But before she ever reached this decision she got bit by the fitness bug and embarked on a healthy eating and exercise plan. She lost her avoirdupois and in the process gained a healthy glow in her face and a great self-image. She is so much more energetic and confident now that she's abandoned all talk of plastic surgery of any kind.

2. ASSESS YOUR SKIN TYPE

Even if you made your regimen gentler just a few years ago, you still might have to fine-tune it a bit more to avoid irritation. As skin matures it continually becomes thinner and drier, which can make it more reactive to products and procedures. If your face feels dry, tight, itchy, has flakes, and/or stings, switch to an extra mild cleanser and a heavier moisturizer for both day and night. To help calibrate your personalized, nonirritating, yet still effective, skin-care regimen, read "Customizing Your Daily Regimen" (pages 71–72).

3. BOLSTER YOUR NATURAL DEFENSES

In addition to using antioxidant-based products mentioned in "Bolster Your Natural Defenses," page 61, to fight free-radical attacks, it is also important to battle our own internal assailants. As we age, the natural enzymes in our skin that erode collagen outpace the mechanisms that build and preserve it. Continually synthesizing collagen through all the measures previously outlined is a key way to combat these destructive forces. But now, especially, protecting the new collagen you create is an even more important step. Both genistein and retinoids have been shown to block the enzymes that tear down collagen and, for this reason, are contained in the M.D. Skincare products. While genistein is completely gentle for all skin types, prescription retinoids, in the form of Renova, can be drying and irritating, even though Renova has a moisturizing base. You may start out with the lowest concentration of Renova and see if you can tolerate it. You can gradually increase its strength if you aren't irritated by it. If you are, drop down to retinol, its nonprescription counterpart.

4. CONSIDER VITAMIN K—TOPICALLY

You might have started to notice that you bruise more easily now than you used to and/or you have under-eye dark circles no matter how much sleep you get. This is because our blood vessels are lined with collagen and as the quality and quantity of it diminishes, they become more fragile and break more easily, which, for the most part, is what causes the bruise or circles. Building collagen will help to strengthen them. Vitamin K (see chapter 8 for more details) can help to protect them from breaking in the first place and heal them once they do. To keep all your bases covered, I recommend applying creams that contain vitamin K topically and including it as part of a balanced diet.

5. GET YOUR VITAMIN B

Biotin, a B vitamin, has been shown to prevent and treat the dry, brittle hair and nails that can occur with age. Chapter 8, pages 163–89, will outline biotin's other benefits and how to incorporate it into your diet.

6. PAMPER YOURSELF

Never underestimate the power of doing things that make you feel better. A massage, pedicure, or regular vacations not only will help you look your best but will also improve your mood and make you more relaxed, which will have an even more profound effect on your appearance than the treatment itself. Rather than Botox or collagen, Bea, seventy, gets her hair done every day as her main beauty boost. She says this little indulgence keeps her looking and feeling more fabulous than any antiaging treatment.

Specialized Treatment for Problem Areas

While it may be more time-consuming and expensive, at this phase in your skin care, taking it slow and steady will truly help you get the results you are looking for. It might be tempting to get a lot of Botox in entrenched forehead lines or extra filler to plump up deep creases in the nasolabial folds. But as skin becomes thinner and more lax, you will get more natural-looking and attractive results by using a bit less of each treatment at one time, which may require doing it a bit more frequently. Treating specific regions of concern, rather than evaluating your face as a whole, may now be a bit more problematic, but this can vary from person to person. If one area becomes wrinkle free while the rest of the face is going through the natural aging process, you might feel that it stands out or looks artificial in comparison.

Then again, you may not care. If you truly have a pet peeve, getting rid of it, and just that, might be all you ever want to do.

Annette, seventy-two, for example, was obsessed about the lines in her forehead and the furrows between her brows. In fact, when she looked in the mirror, they were the only things she saw. So she decided to go for it. We used Botox optimally to give her the relaxed, more youthful-looking forehead she had wanted but did nothing else for any of her other signs of aging. (See photo section, page 6.) She is completely happy with her appearance and isn't even contemplating getting Botox or anything else, for that matter, in any other part of her face.

Objectively speaking, there may be just one or two areas that do look older than the rest of your face. In fact, treating these features and just these features may be all you have to do to turn back the clock. Virginia, fifty-five, was stupendous looking—genetically blessed with a gorgeous, youthful complexion except for the lines she had around her mouth; they literally looked at least ten years older than the rest of her face. Because they bothered her so much, she became very critical of her appearance and kept suggesting fairly aggressive full-face treatments, as well as Botox and soft-tissue fillers—everywhere. I pointed out to her that the rest of her face was fantastic, and there was absolutely no need to fix what wasn't broken. Instead, we decided to go all out and just tackle her real issue—the lines around her mouth. We did deep CO_2 laser resurfacing just in that area. She rode out all the oozing, weepiness, and redness. The procedure was a total success and three years later, she is still delighted with the way she looks and has stopped talking about doing anything unnecessary to her face. It also doesn't hurt that most people are incredulous when she tells them she is fifty-five and not, in fact, in her mid-forties!

So whether you want to rejuvenate just one feature, several, or your whole face, as always, the first step is to try the less aggressive strategies already outlined. If you've progressed to the measures outlined in Level Three (chapter 5), and still want more of a change, here are some more aggressive antiaging methods for you to consider:

GOING DEEPER WITH PEELS, LASERS, AND DERMABRASION TO SMOOTH OUT AND TIGHTEN LAX SKIN, WHILE SPURRING COLLAGEN

Because of its recovery time and its possible complications, deep resurfacing is considered to be one of the big guns in the antiaging arsenal. It is performed either with a laser, a peel, or a dermabrasion machine. Like their medium counterparts, deep laser and peel resurfacing burn off damaged skin to erase many of the signs of time. Dermabrasion uses a mechanism that sands off the damaged surface. This controlled injury causes new collagen to form as the skin heals, making a face look smoother and more youthful looking as a result. Depending on the amount of damage prior to the procedure and the skin type, deep resurfacing can substantially reduce—even actually eliminate—lines in the upper lip, forehead, and crow's-feet area. It is excellent for crinkling and will lighten sunspots. It is sometimes also used as a means to remove precancerous growths called keratoses. You still may want Botox to prevent wear and tear in certain areas, soft-tissue fillers in deeper indentations, sessions with a YAG laser to completely remove brown spots, and light peels to help maintain your results and further stimulate collagen production. While it is not a magic bullet, deep resurfacing does treat several different issues simultaneously and offers long-lasting results, making the face look fresher and revitalized overall.

When considering deep resurfacing, it is important to keep in mind that, while it will have somewhat of an overall firming effect on your face, it cannot tighten severe sagging, erase entrenched forehead wrinkles, smooth out deep creases in the nasolabial folds, or eliminate eye bags. If you crank up any of these treatments to the intensity where they could literally remove excess sagging skin, the risks would far outweigh the benefits. Sagging is best tackled through surgical tightening. And in fact, deep resurfacing is often performed simultaneously with a face-lift to correct fine lines in the crow's-feet and upper lip, since a face-lift only re-drapes and pulls drooping skin but doesn't affect overall texture.

The degree of improvement depends on the strength of the peel, laser, or dermabrasion machine; the depth they penetrate; and the extent of the damage before treatment. But the greater the intensity of the procedure, the greater its potential hazards. There is more than a 75 percent chance that deep resurfacing treatments will cause hyperpigmentation or hypopigmentation in people with medium, olive, Asian, and darker skin tones. Scarring is another potential side effect. Frequently, these conditions are permanent and cannot be concealed with makeup, especially in areas that have been overlapped. Ultra fair-skinned people with light eyes and blond hair are, for now, the best candidates for deep resurfacing. However, other skin tones can achieve good results if they don't push for perfection and the doctor is conservative and extremely skilled at performing the procedure. Plus, some people prefer some slightly hypopigmented areas to lines and wrinkles. It is a trade-off, so it's up to you to decide which issues bother you the most and which ones you can live with.

Because they are quite invasive with a lot of recovery time, these procedures are generally performed once in a lifetime though, in some rare instances, they might be administered twice several years apart. All of them are performed under local anesthetic and may be combined with intravenous sedation to make you drowsy and calm. To prevent infection, your doctor will give you prescriptions for an antibiotic and an antiviral medication to help prevent infection as well as cortisone to help prevent swelling and advise you when and for how long you should take each one.

The recovery time with all three of these treatments is substantial though it does vary with skin type, your own natural healing abilities, and the depth of the procedure. Typically, skin is oozing, weepy, bright red, and painful for one week afterward. For another one to three weeks, skin will remain a bright red that makeup typically cannot cover. After that, skin can stay unnaturally pink for up to two months, but you should be able to conceal it fairly well with makeup. I recommend you wait till any redness completely recedes before using any products other than a gentle cleanser, sunscreen, and a fragrance-free and oil-free moisturizer. It is also especially important to avoid sun exposure, which can cause hyperpigmentation in recently resurfaced skin, and to wear at least an SPF 30 whenever you are outside.

While the aftermath of a deep resurfacing treatment may seem frightening enough to make you question someone's sanity, none of my patients have ever regretted undergoing it even throughout the difficult healing process. Anna, fifty-two, for example, wanted to diminish the appearance of the lines above her upper lip and in the crow's-feet area. Nonablative lasers, Botox around her eyes, and peels weren't giving her completely satisfactory results. A plastic surgeon advised her that if she got a face-lift for those areas, she also would need substantial work on her neck so it would be in sync with her newly lifted face. Since two surgeries weren't an attractive option for her, we discussed doing a deep CO_2 laser treatment. Because of her skin type and the sensitivity of those two areas, we opted to do a full-face treatment rather than treat each area separately so they wouldn't stand out from the rest of her face due to hypopigmentation. While I was fairly aggressive in treating her regions of concern, I could make the laser less intense to treat her less damaged areas. After the challenging healing process, her skin was radiant, more even toned, and less lined. Her skin looked fabulous, and she was delighted with the results. The procedure did lighten her skin tone a bit but since it was a global and not a regional change, she actually preferred it to her original skin tone and merely lightened her hair to accommodate the change. Seven years later, she is still extremely pleased.

Deep Laser Resurfacing

The most common laser used in deep resurfacing treatments is the carbon dioxide (CO_2) laser turned up higher than when used in medium resurfacing. The laser is passed over the face to remove the skin's surface and its accompanying lines, soft wrinkles, crinkling, and sun damage. In the process, your skin's fibroblasts are stimulated into producing collagen to "heal" the areas the laser has removed.

Deep Chemical Peels

At the end of the day, peels aren't that much different from laser resurfacing except that their destruction of the damaged skin is chemical rather than heat induced. The chemical solution eliminates a part of the sun damage and new collagen forms as part of the healing process. The type of acid, the lower its pH, and the longer it is left on your skin will determine how dramatic the results, how long the recovery, and the risk of side effects. The degree of improvement also depends on the extent of the damage before treatment.

For decades, phenol was the deep chemical peel of choice. But with the advent of laser resurfacing, and the somewhat milder yet nearly as effective trichloroacetic acid (TCA), most dermatologists and plastic surgeons no longer use it. The reason? In more cases than not, phenol peels significantly depigment the skin, leaving behind stark lines of demarcation at the edges of the face where the therapy ended. Phenol peels can also cause scarring and be toxic to the body. It has been associated with cardiac arrhythmia, especially in people with prior heart conditions. Most dermatologists and plastic surgeons that perform deep peels now use a TCA solution at a stronger concentration than the one used for a medium peel since it has been shown to have fewer complications and not carry the health risks of phenol.

Dermabrasion

Because it is the most aggressive and the least controllable of the three options, dermabrasion isn't as popular as it once was, but it is still used by some doctors. The procedure involves either a wire brush or a burr containing diamond particles attached to a motorized handle (it looks like a dentist's drill) that scrapes away the skin's surface to make a wrinkle less visible. With dermabrasion, there seems to be the most opportunity for overlapping, which can lead to permanent linear scars and severe hypopigmentation. But if you have very fair and severely damaged skin, it might be an effective option for you.

Making a Choice

While all three resurfacing procedures have similar downtimes and nearly the same risks, I find the laser to be far more beneficial and less likely to cause complications than the other two methods since it is more versatile and easier to control. For example, with the medium laser, you can turn it up a bit higher to treat more damaged areas and then gradually taper it back down for less damaged ones. With a peel and dermabrasion, your only option is to rub or press harder in some areas than others, which will undoubtedly increase your risk of scarring, hypopigmentation or hyperpigmentation, and uneven results. It is important to discuss these concerns with your doctor so he can help you decide your specific needs and what will work the best for you. Whichever procedure you agree upon, make sure your doctor is extremely experienced and adept at performing it.

Spot Treatment

If you are only troubled by one particular area of your face and it has not responded to less invasive products and procedures, it is possible to have a deep resurfacing treatment on just one region, such as the crow's-feet or the lines around the mouth. This will definitely cut back on some of the downtime. The greatest risk with regional resurfacing is that the treated area may look out of sync with the rest of your face—either because it looks younger or because there is a noticeable change in skin pigmentation. It is, however, a plausible and highly effective solution in some cases.

FACE-LIFTS FOR DEEP CREASES IN THE NASOLABIAL FOLDS, GENERAL SAGGING

If you've tried all the less invasive measures outlined in chapters 3, 4, and 5 and still want to make more of a change, it may be time for you to consider some form of cosmetic surgery. The only way to really eliminate and firm sagging skin, so far, is to remove some of it and pull the rest tighter. While a face-lift (technically known as rhytidectomy) can't stop time dead in its tracks, it can improve some of the most visible signs of aging by eliminating excess fat, tightening muscles, and redistributing the skin of your face.

Performed either with local anesthesia and a sedative, or under general anesthesia, depending on patient and doctor preference, the surgery involves the surgeon first making an incision above the hairline at the temples, then extending it in a natural line in front of the ear (or just inside the cartilage at the front of the ear), and continuing behind the earlobe to the lower scalp. If you decide you'd also like some work done on your neck, a small incision may also be made under the chin. In general, the surgeon separates the skin from the fat and muscle below. Fat may be trimmed or suctioned from around the neck and chin to create more definition. The surgeon then tightens the underlying muscle, pulls the skin back, and removes the excess.

Recovery time and postoperative pain vary. In general, bandages, if used, are typically removed after several days. Stitches are removed in five to seven days. Your face may be pale, bruised, and puffy for a few weeks; and your skin will feel somewhat tender and numb. You may feel tired and not quite yourself for a week. Your doctor will give you specific guidelines about when you can return to work, resume normal activities, and engage in vigorous ones. But expect to be at home resting for around ten days to two weeks.

You will have some permanent scars as a result of the operation, but a skillful surgeon can conceal them in your hair or in the natural creases of your face and/or ears, and they usually fade over time. Complications from a face-lift may include hematoma (a collection of blood under the skin), nerve damage, infection, and reactions to the anesthesia.

Less of a Lift

If your concerns are mostly in the lower half of your face—e.g., the nasolabial folds, jawline, and your cheeks—you may be a candidate for a minilift, a procedure in which the skin and tissue are redraped only from the midface to the neck. Because the incision can be smaller and less of an area is being operated on, recovery time and risks can be greatly reduced.

A new procedure utilizing one or two stitches buried below the skin to simply lift the face is pending FDA approval. This so-called Feather Lift may work well, especially to reduce the nasolabial fold, but only time will tell.

When seeking a dramatic change, a full face-lift or even a minilift aren't your only options. You can ask the doctor to be more moderate and pull less tightly and then use injectible fillers to plump up any remaining depressions. Employing this strategy may bring you closer to looking like a more youthful-looking you. If you look at pictures of yourself when you were younger, your face wasn't just more taut; it was also fuller and plumper. If you decide to use a more permanent filler such as silicone or Artecoll, have them administered *after* the surgery because if done before surgery, these fillers may protrude once the skin is pulled more tightly over them.

Another procedure that lifts sagging cheeks and reduces the appearance of deep groves in the nasolabial folds is the Gore-Tex cheek lift. In this type of lift, the doctor weaves Gore-Tex threads under the fat pads in the cheeks, then knots them, lifting the fat up and out. When gravity exerts its pull again, the ends of the thread can be pulled taut. Most experts agree that this procedure is best reserved for younger women in their forties and fifties who have less sagging and laxity in their muscles.

While it may seem wildly premature to even consider a face-lift or any type of lifting procedure when you are not even fifty, in some cases, it may be an appropriate choice. Susan, from Florida, was an avid fan of outdoor water sports and of going up north to ski. When she was thirty-eight, she realized that she was heading down the same path as her mother with prematurely sagging skin and deep creases in the nasolabial folds that would only get more pronounced over time. Most people, in fact, typically thought she was in her late forties. Much to the protestations of her friends and family who thought she was "way too young" to undergo this operation, she went for it and got a "light" face-lift. She is now forty-five and is being mistaken for thirty-five.

But even if you see yourself repeating your family patterns of premature aging, getting a face-lift when you are too young can lead to disappointing results. Joanne was a huge sun worshiper and decided to get a face-lift in her forties because she felt she looked much older than her peers. She was very unhappy with the results, either because she was not an appropriate candidate for the surgery or she was pulled too tightly. She came to me at sixty-seven because despite the face-lift, she had continued to show dramatic signs of aging, the result of her continuing to sunbathe regularly. We did everything we could to improve her skin's texture and firmness, but we were not getting the results she wanted. She was terrified to get another face-lift but was severely unhappy with her appearance. I explained to her that she was probably much more of a candidate for the operation now than she was in her forties and that she should find a surgeon with a more natural-looking aesthetic. She did just that and is extremely happy with the results of this second go-round.

Even Less of a Lift

Permanent Gore-Tex or silicone surgical implants in the cheeks and/or chin is another way to provide somewhat of a lift to sagging skin, but that's not their main purpose. It's actually to add volume and definition to areas that you feel need augmentation—tweaking what your were born with, so to speak, rather than turning back the clock (though some age-related changes can be helped too). Implants do hold up soft tissue to some extent and provide contour to less defined areas, which can lead to a more youthful appearance. But implants do not correct sagging or prevent it from occurring. In fact, many surgeons who are doing chin implant surgery perform a neck lift or lipectomy simultaneously to help create more definition.

Since these implants are permanent, it is far better to create higher, more chiseled cheekbones or a stronger chin later rather than sooner. There's no telling how the rest of your face will hold up around them, and if you decide you'd like to have any kind of plastic surgery later on, they can pop out and look unnatural under newly tightened skin. Should you become unhappy with an implant, removing it requires another surgery, which can cause scarring and other complications.

A surgical implant is imbedded immediately under the skin through a very small incision. Typically the procedure is performed under local anesthesia and intravenous sedation. One of its main drawbacks is that all types of implants can be felt and oftentimes seen through the skin. Silicone rubber is said to look and feel more natural than Gore-Tex, however. In addition, cheek implant surgery can yield asymmetrical results and an implant can shift up or down over time, both of which may require additional surgery to correct the problem. There is also a risk of infection, which will necessitate the implant's removal. If this is the case, you and your surgeon will decide if it's worthwhile to replace it. My observation, overall, is that individuals are happy with their implants when the surgery is performed by a meticulous and skillful plastic surgeon.

SAGGING NECK AND JOWLS

Three things can actually cause a sagging neck: excess skin, excess fat, and/or lax muscles. If you are not getting the results that you want from light peels, antiaging products, and Botox injections, there is a group of surgical procedures to get right to the heart of your specific problems. You can have cervicoplasty to remove the excess skin, platysmaplasty to tighten or alter muscles, and/or lipectomy, basically neck liposuction to remove excess fat.

In plastysmaplasty surgery, the surgeon first makes incisions under your neck and behind your ears in order to have access to the platysma muscle and tighten it. Permanent sutures may be used to hold it into place. Sometimes part of the muscle is removed. But, as discussed, Botox injections can be a satisfactory alternative to this particular procedure (pages 79–84).

If your concern is excess fat, your surgeon will make a small incision below the chin and suction it out as with liposuction. For too much skin, he will make similar incisions for a cervicoplasty: one behind each ear and one under the chin, trimming parts of the skin and lifting it into place. The anesthesia used will depend on both you and your doctor's personal preferences, how much work you want done, and your comfort level.

Recovery time varies but generally you will be instructed to wear a compression bandage for about a week. Swelling and bruising can last for several days. Sensations of tightness, burning, pulling, tingling, or numbness can last for up to a few weeks. Most people can return to work in ten to fourteen days but will most likely have to wait about a month to resume more vigorous activities.

FOREHEAD

If your forehead is your main area of concern, you might be tempted to consider a forehead lift or brow lift—especially if you've been regularly incorporating the less aggressive remedies outlined in chapters 3, 4, and 5 and are still not happy with the way it looks. But before you take the plunge, it is important to note that a brow lift is considered to be one of the most painful and invasive forms of plastic surgery with a high rate of patient dissatisfaction. In addition, lately, its longevity has also been called into question. Though more studies are required, it may not be the permanent fix it was once thought to be. Many plastic surgeons now actually prefer to administer Botox rather than to perform brow lifts. According to the American Society of Plastic Surgeons, from the year 2000 to 2003, the number of brow lifts performed declined by 52 percent, while the number of Botox injections administered by plastic surgeons increased by 267 percent.

Should you decide you would like the permanence and lower regular maintenance of forehead surgery versus quarterly Botox injections, it is important to discuss your expectations with your surgeon. Do you want to have a perfectly tight, smooth forehead and risk looking unnatural, or are you willing to live with some imperfections in order to preserve a more natural look? A common complaint with forehead lifts is that the brows get positioned too high up leading to a permanently startled expression.

You should also address the possibility that a surgically corrected forehead may look out of sync with the rest of your face since, in some cases, it will look more taut and less lined than other areas. For this reason, forehead lifts are often performed in conjunction with a full face-lift—the idea being that this way your entire face appears smoother and more youthful, rather than just one region. This necessity for having additional surgery may be the deal breaker for you—or you may decide to go for it all. Another possibility is that you decide that you are so bothered by your forehead that you don't care if it looks younger than the rest of your face.

In a forehead lift, the muscles and tissues that cause the furrowing or drooping are removed or tightened to smooth the forehead, raise the eyebrows, and minimize frown lines. You should discuss the merits of having the procedure done endoscopically—when a tube-shaped probe (called an endoscope) is inserted through three tiny incisions at the hairline to permit the surgeon to see and perform the entire procedure. Typically endoscopic surgery involves less postoperative swelling, bruising, scarring, and discomfort. Most forehead lifts are performed under local anesthesia, combined with a sedative, though depending on patience preference and the amount of surgery, in some cases general anesthesia is used.

Healing time varies from person to person but downtime may include swelling in the forehead, cheeks, and eyes for about a week along with numbness on the top of the scalp. As the nerves heal, the numbness is generally replaced by itching, which may last for as long as six months. Endoscopic forehead-surgery patients usually experience less of the numbness and itching than classic forehead lift patients. Some of the hair around your incision may fall out and may temporarily be a bit thinner, but normal growth usually resumes within a few weeks or months. Permanent hair loss is an extremely rare, though possible, complication.

Most patients are back to work in a week to ten days, with most visible signs of the surgery fading completely after about three weeks. You will probably be advised to limit or avoid vigorous physical activity for several weeks. Prolonged exposure to heat or sun also should be limited for several months.

Permanent complications are rare and may include injury to the nerves that control eyebrow movement on one or both sides resulting in an inability to raise the eyebrows or wrinkle the forehead. Formation of a broad, highly visible scar is also a rare complication, but it generally has to be surgically removed so that a new thinner scar grows in its place.

LINES AROUND THE MOUTH AND THINNING LIPS

Increasingly, I find more and more of my patients frustrated that as they mature, their lips start to thin out, and the area above their mouths becomes heavily lined. But even if the lines are firmly entrenched, less aggressive, noninvasive treatments, such as nonablative laser sessions, light peels, and a good solid skincare regimen with proven antiaging ingredients, such as vitamin C, retinol, and exfoliating acids, can help to smooth them out and make them less visible. If you haven't yet tried any of these measures outlined in chapters 3, 4, and 5, embarking on them now can make a difference and prevent more damage tomorrow. The next step might be to try an injectible filler to plump up the lines and add volume to your lips (see chapters 4 and 5 for specifics). So far, the more permanent fillers such as silicone, Artecoll, and Radiance have not proven themselves to be satisfactory at either augmenting thinning lips or filling in the lines above them. Studies have shown that their results are uneven, bumpy and/or hard. It is also possible to have lips surgically augmented with implants; but in general, this procedure is rife with complications such as infection, undue hardness, shifting, and a condition where the implant literally pokes through the side of the mouth (more common with Gore-Tex implants). For now, the temporary fillers (Restylane, Perlane and Collagen) truly seem to offer the best results.

For lines around the mouth, there are many more options. If, after peels, nonablative laser sessions, and fillers, you still want more of an improvement, you can try a medium laser resurfacing treatment (done before you get a filler) outlined in chapter 5 or a deeper one for more substantial grooves (see page 135).

There are also a few minor tricks that can help return your smile to its former energetic and ebullient state. As we age, we often get deep creases on the sides of the mouth that make it look like it's sloping downward all the time—almost like a perpetual frown. I find that injecting a very small amount of Botox ¼ inch below the lower lip at the outer corners allows it to slope upward in a more natural looking (read: happier-looking) curve. Again, being conservative is key. If too much Botox is used, it can result in your not being able to smile properly or close your mouth all the way. But if your doctor is skilled in the art of Botox correction, it shouldn't be a problem.

BAGGY UPPER AND LOWER EYELIDS

Both the upper and lower eyelids are fairly tricky areas to treat. The problems that usually arise there are due to excess or lax skin or the shape and thickness of the fat pads under the eyes. These issues, then, cannot be treated with Botox or fillers and cannot be dramatically helped with medium or deep resurfacing treatments. You can improve your eyelids' appearance by building collagen stores and safeguarding your skin against free radicals as discussed in the first three levels.

One of the biggest issues for my patients with sagging eyelids is that they feel that their eyes look smaller because their upper lid droops over them. This is a common complaint, and there actually is an easy, noninvasive and fast-acting solution for it. I have had reasonably good results in "opening up" eyes by using a tiny amount of Botox. One shot is injected 1 to 2 mm below the lower lid line, just in line with the pupil, to open up the lower lid, thus creating a more open eye. The one caveat with this technique is the doctor needs to be extremely precise in administering the Botox to avoid opening it up too much or you *temporarily* won't be able to close your eyes all the way.

Plastic surgery, on the other hand, is *permanent*. And that sometimes can have its merits. If you've tried all the noninvasive strategies outlined in the previous chapters and are still not happy with the appearance of your eyes, you may want to take the plunge and consider a blepharoplasty to remove fat along with excess skin from the upper and lower eyelids. In general, the surgical community regards blepharoplasties as one of the most risk-free procedures that deliver the most satisfying results, though they are not completely without complications. Blepharoplasties are usually performed on an outpatient basis under local anesthesia along with oral or intravenous sedatives.

In a typical procedure, the surgeon makes incisions in the creases of the upper lids and just below the lashes in the lower lids. The incisions may extend into the crow's-feet at the outer corners of your eyes. Working through these incisions, the surgeon separates the skin from underlying fatty tissue and muscle and removes excess fat and trims sagging skin. The incisions are closed with very fine sutures. Often, this procedure is combined with deep laser resurfacing to remove fine lines at the same time. If you and your surgeon decide that this is an appropriate course of action for you, be sure to discuss your risks of hypopigmentation and the other complications that can result from deep laser resurfacing (see above for more specifics).

Following the surgery, you will be instructed to keep your head elevated for several days and to use cold compresses to reduce swelling and bruising, which can last anywhere from two weeks to a month. Your eyes also may be dry, burn, itch, tear, be sensitive to light, or have blurred vision for the first few weeks. Some people may not be able to close their eyes totally when they sleep, which in rare cases can be permanent. Another very rare complication, which can only be corrected with more surgery is ectropion, when the lower lids pull downward. A more common occurrence is when too much fat is taken out from the lower lid resulting in a hollow, almost skeletal appearance under the eyes. Discussing these concerns with your surgeon can minimize the risks of them occurring as some are related to the degree of correction you seek.

If you have under-eye puffiness without sagging and choose to surgically eliminate it, you might be a good candidate for a subconjunctival blepharoplasty. This procedure is usually performed on younger patients with thicker, more elastic skin. Less invasive than a traditional blepharoplasty and with far less downtime, the surgeon makes just a tiny incision on the inside of the eyelid using a scalpel and then excises the excess fat causing the puffiness. The area is then cauterized to stop the bleeding. Because the procedure requires such a small incision and the bleeding is minimal, there is seldom, if any, scarring and only a tiny amount of bruising immediately afterward. The bruising generally can be covered with makeup and subsides in a week or less.

Sometimes, eyelid surgery positively can affect other features, as well. Jean, sixty, for example, got her upper and lower eyelids done so she could better address the issue that was really bothering her—the lines and furrows in her forehead. Because her eyelids drooped (which didn't thrill her all that much either), I could never use Botox optimally to smooth her forehead because it would have made her lids sag further. Instead of opting for the painful and risky brow-lift surgery to make her happier with her forehead, she decided on the far less invasive and less chancy blepharoplasty surgery. Once her lids no longer sagged, we could use enough Botox to completely correct her forehead lines. The surgery, in effect, tackled two problems simultaneously and allowed her to take a less aggressive approach that still provided dramatic and satisfying results.

Whichever route you choose to go—be it surgical, topical, in-office procedures, or a combination—now, more than ever, is the time to make decisions for yourself. It can be trickier these days to be happy with the way you look when other women your age look younger due to plastic surgery. But it is important to remember that while plastic surgery may turn back the clock, it may alter your features so you just don't quite look like yourself anymore, which may be a welcome change for many. Decide what you want to look like and act upon it. Do you want to look your natural self only somewhat younger, less tired, and more refreshed? If so, then antiaging products and in-office procedures are sufficient. If you want to look much younger and accept the risk of looking different from your previous self, then plastic surgery may be your best option. Sometimes a combination of both options is the best approach.

The most exciting part of being in Level Four? *Any* change you make will clearly be seen. There is so much you can do to get and/or maintain beautiful healthy-looking skin.

7
Beauty Bonus Points

14 SUREFIRE LIFESTYLE HABITS FOR HEALTHIER AND YOUNGER-LOOKING SKIN

When it comes to our skin, maintaining a balanced diet and overall healthy lifestyle are guarantees. If you do, there is no question that you will look better than if you don't. Of course you can't "be perfect" all the time. The goal, here, is to make deposits in your beauty bank by drinking enough water and getting enough sleep, among others, to outweigh the withdrawals, such as smoking, drinking to excess, and sunbathing. Racking up beauty bonus points will also help you to better withstand an occasional splurge and to make up for some of the factors that are beyond your control; for example, your past sun exposure and lifestyle habits, and your genetics. Here, in no particular order, are the healthy habits that I have found in all my years of practice to be the most crucial to the health and appearance of my patient's skin.

1. GET ENOUGH SLEEP

Truly this is easier said than done for those of us who not only never seem to have sufficient hours in the day but also have enough stress to keep us wide awake when we finally do crawl into bed. Think of how you look and feel when you come home from a vacation where you finally managed to "catch up." Imagine looking and feeling that way all the time! The reason chronic lack of sleep (and to a lesser extent occasional sleepless nights) affects us so negatively is because the body responds to it by setting off our fight-or-flight response because it sees our intense fatigue as a mild state of emergency. The production of the stress hormones cortisol and epinepherine (a.k.a. adrenaline) are triggered, which then prompts the body to divert a disproportionate amount of blood flow, oxygen, and nutrients away from our external organ (i.e., the skin) to the major internal ones, such as the heart, brain, and kidneys. When the skin is getting less than optimum fuel, it can become dull and pale with dark under-eye circles. Lack of sleep can be so stressful that it actually causes our bodies, including our skin, to generate free radicals.

You might also find that not getting your beauty sleep results in lines and wrinkles looking more firmly entrenched. The reason? Our sympathetic nervous system involuntarily contracts our muscles in response to the overall stress the body is experiencing. Think about how tight your neck and shoulders can get when you are really stressed out. In the case of our faces, when our muscles are contracted, such as when we clench our jaws or furrow our foreheads, our problem areas become more pronounced.

2. KICK THE HABIT

Smoking is like a triple whammy to our overall health and to our skin. First off, tar triggers free radicals, which can cause cancer as well as break down collagen. Secondly, nicotine disrupts sleep because it is a stimulant. Ever notice how cigarettes can make you feel hyper? It's the nicotine that makes our heart race, which is also what ultimately contributes to heart disease. Nicotine also mimics the effects that stress hormones have on the body by sending it into a flight-or-fight mode. Lastly, smoking ages the skin around the mouth because, next to the lungs, the mouth is the prime recipient of the toxins in secondhand smoke. Meanwhile, regularly pursing the lips to take a puff causes enough wear and tear to create smoker's lines—pleats around the lips that eventually become visible even when you're not smoking. (See photo section, page 3.)

3. SWITCH TO A SATIN PILLOWCASE

While it may make some people snore, sleeping on our backs (something I can't do) is actually the best position to help preserve a youthful-looking complexion. In fact, stomach and side sleepers (especially those who favor the same side every night) actually run the risk of getting lines as a result of their nocturnal habits. This is because persistently pressing our faces into a pillow causes trauma to the skin. Over time, this trauma, aggravated by the friction of a cotton pillowcase, can create permanent creases as our collagen breaks down. In addition, the weight of our own faces impairs circulation to the part we have pressed into the pillow, which compromises the skin's regenerative abilities. If you cannot sleep on your back, which takes the pressure completely off the face, try covering your pillow with a satin pillowcase to minimize friction.

While there still can be a slight amount of abrasion, the skin will slide more easily over satin than cotton. The women in the 1950s who slept on satin pillowcases to protect their hairdos were really onto something!

4. EXERCISE REGULARLY

Not working out doesn't just affect our waistlines, it can also show up in our faces. The American Heart Association recommends a minimum of thirty to sixty minutes of vigorous activity (if you are fit), at 50 to 70 percent of your maximum heart rate on most days of the week if you want to exceed a moderate level of fitness, which has been shown to have increased health benefits. But moderate-level activities often will help lower your health risks to some extent. When our cardiovascular system is functioning optimally we have proper circulation, which ensures the optimum flow of blood and nutrients to the skin. Working out just before an important event is also one of the beauty secrets of those who regularly walk the red carpet. Because exercising (cardio in particular) revs up the circulatory system, it not only imparts the face with a radiant glow but it also mobilizes any trapped fluids so puffy areas usually deflate dramatically and remain that way for at least several hours afterward. Sweating also helps to release any water that your body may be unnecessarily retaining. Just don't overdo high impact, skin-damaging aerobic activities.

5. GIVE THOSE KNEES A REST

High impact exercise, especially running, may result in fabulous legs, but it can negatively impact the skin. It has been my observation that most die-hard runners have premature lines, wrinkles, and sagging. I'm fairly certain that their damaged skin is not just due to the sun but also to the constant pounding their bodies are subjected to. Newton's third law of physics explains it best: "For every action, there is an equal opposite reaction." This means that if a 130-pound woman's foot strikes a surface, the force of 130 pounds bounces back off the ground and up into her body. I believe this jostling not only can damage joints but also can cause collagen breakdown. If you are a passionate runner and are concerned about your skin, try alternating your runs with lower impact forms of exercise, such as walking, the Stairmaster, bike, or Elliptical Cross Trainer. While it may be a four-letter word to marathoners, some running coaches actually counsel their clients to walk one minute for every mile they run to save their joints and, believe it or not, help improve their time. And I have many patients who have switched from running to fast walking and love it.

6. LIMIT EXPOSURE TO EXTREME TEMPERATURES

The signs posted outside steam rooms, saunas, and Jacuzzis recommend that you spend no longer than ten to twenty minutes basking in their warmth. This guideline is given to prevent the complications that could arise from their affect on blood pressure or other medical conditions. But keeping this time limit in mind can also have positive effects on skin. Prolonged exposure to excessive heat can break down our collagen and elastin and cause broken capillaries. In addition, extremely high temperatures can also speed up the breakdown of injectible antiaging fillers such as collagen, Perlane, and Restylane, as well as reduce the longevity of Botox.

Excessive *cold*, on the other hand, can also cause broken capillaries. When we are freezing, our body attempts to conserve heat internally by constricting the blood vessels on the skin's surface so that it becomes shortchanged of the nutrients, blood flow, and oxygen it needs. In response to this stress, our skin produces more vessels in an attempt to supply it with more blood flow. If you are an avid skier, prone to broken capillaries, and concerned about your skin, you can help prevent further damage by wrapping a scarf around your face or wearing a ski mask when temperatures are especially frigid.

7. MAINTAIN A STABLE WEIGHT

"At some point in your life, you have to choose between your face and your rear end," is a parable frequently printed in fashion magazines. And it's actually true. In my experience, people who have repeatedly gained and lost substantial amounts of weight over their lifetime, or lose more than 5 percent from a healthy body weight beyond middle age, will most likely look older than those who haven't. Weight gain of any kind stretches the skin, which stresses the collagen and elastin fibers. As we age, our skin has less of an ability to snap back into shape when we lose the weight that caused it to expand in the first place. I've had patients in their fifties whose faces looked great until they lost a significant amount of weight. Then, all of a sudden they looked like they needed a face-lift because their skin couldn't recoil back far enough. It's better for our faces to lose weight in our twenties and thirties while our skin is still elastic. After that, it may not be a bad idea to lose weight gradually while evaluating the effects it is having on your face. It's generally a trade-off, but it's up to *you,* not what the media or your peers dictate, to decide which matters more to you. While you may want to lose twenty pounds to fit back into a favorite article of clothing, your face might look more youthful if you limit your weight loss to ten pounds. Similarly, you might prefer having an extra svelte figure to a fuller face. Both are attractive options.

8. TRY TO KEEP A REGULAR SCHEDULE WHEN TRAVELING

Our body has its own natural, or circadian, rhythm for its wake-sleep cycles. It typically produces our highest amount of the regulatory hormone cortisol, which gives us energy and alertness, at 8:00 A.M. and the lowest amount at 4:00 P.M. This dip in cortisol is why we often feel lethargic in the afternoon and start to crave a candy bar or a cup of coffee to give us a shot of energy. Jet lag disrupts this natural rhythm so that we end up producing cortisol when we don't need it. When our body is in this state, the stress hormones become activated and produce the same effects as when we are in fight-or-flight mode. I find that one way to counteract jet lag is to make small adjustments geared to the time zone you are in. For example, when I fly from New York to L.A., I try to keep myself awake till 10:00 P.M. L.A. time (1:00 A.M. New York time) and then I am generally able to sleep till 6: 00 A.M. (9:00 A.M. New York time). Every night thereafter, I seem to be able to stay awake a little bit longer and sleep a little bit later. But you know your body best. So you may even have your own jet lag remedies. The important thing here is to try and get enough sleep whenever you can, wherever you are.

9. TRAVEL WITH YOUR OWN WATER

It's not only the water that we drink that can affect our skin, it's also the water with which we wash our faces. I have patients who travel and return from their trips with blemishes, rosacea, excessive shine, or irritation that they didn't have before. I believe this is because the tap water in their hotels has different minerals from the water coming out of the faucets in their homes. If skin is not accustomed to certain minerals, they may cause adverse reactions. I have found that the best way to combat this travel-related skin problem is to simply pack an Evian mister or a spray bottle filled with tap water from your home when you travel. Use either one to rinse off your face after you cleanse with the local water.

10. AVOID ALCOHOL-BASED SKIN-CARE PRODUCTS

Applying alcohol topically can dehydrate skin, break blood vessels, exacerbate rosacea and eczema, plus trap skin in a vicious cycle. Because it dries out skin, alcohol can prod it to produce more oil to help lubricate it, which may then lead you to use even more of the alcohol-based toner. Eventually the skin becomes over-stripped so the alcohol-based product has the ability to penetrate more deeply than it is supposed to, which can cause the type of irritation that can lead to broken capillaries.

If you like to use a toner—whether to control excess shine, remove cleansing residue, or exfoliate—switch to one that is witch hazel–based, which does all of the above without stripping.

11. REMOVE MAKEUP BEFORE GOING TO BED

Hitting the sheets "made up" can clog pores and oil glands, which is almost a surefire ticket to blemishes and irritations. In addition, once the makeup becomes impacted in pores, it can actually stretch them out and make them appear larger. Once makeup and other pore-clogging gunk is removed, pores usually shrink back to their original size. But as we mature and our collagen production declines, stretched out pores no longer completely snap back into shape and so become permanently enlarged.

12. BE GENTLE

Exfoliating with rough, grainy, scrubs, or scouring skin with your fingernails while cleansing can cause irritation, and broken blood vessels. It will also aggravate acne, rosacea, eczema, and seborrheic dermatitis. If you prefer to use an exfoliating scrub, look for ones that incorporate smooth, round, polyethylene beads versus products with rough, jagged nuts, seeds, husks, kernels, or pits.

13. WEAR SUNGLASSES

Because the skin under and around our eyes is especially thin, any damage to this region shows up faster than anywhere else on the face and is particularly noticeable. Sunglasses serve as a physical barrier to block out the ultraviolet rays and so help to prevent the signs of premature aging. Wearing sunglasses also helps stop us from squinting, which causes wear and tear around the eyes and in between brows. When selecting a pair of sunglasses, think SUNGLASSES—Big, round, full coverage glasses that sit firmly and high enough on the bridge of the nose so there is minimal space between your face and the frames for the sun to penetrate. Jackie O got it right, and she was not only a fashion icon but she also had lovely skin. And make sure your big round fashionable lenses have been treated with a broad-spectrum (UVA/UVB) protective coating.

14. WEAR SUNSCREEN AND LOTS OF IT

Safeguarding your skin against the sun is the single most important thing you can do for your skin's health and appearance. And if you are using products that increase your photosensitivity, such as Renova, it's doubly important. It's so important, in fact, that even though it's been said millions and millions of times, it's always worth repeating: Wear sunscreen and lots of it. An SPF 30 is optimal.

8

THE RECIPE FOR GORGEOUS SKIN

We may not be able to control our genetics or the lifestyle habits we had in the past, but we can monitor what we eat; and the payoffs of a healthy diet are amazing. Eating well is one of the easiest, least expensive, and guaranteed ways to achieve and maintain radiant and beautiful skin—not to mention what it will do for the rest of your body. I consider it another health and beauty bonus point. For this chapter, I enlisted my friend Caren Feingold, RD, a New York City nutritionist in private practice to compile a list of some of the most important nutrients for skin (and your overall health, by the way). To my mind, there are six rules of thumb that will help put you on the path to amazing-looking skin:

1. THINK HEALTHY HEART, HEALTHY SKIN

All the foods we've been told to eat and to avoid for the prevention of heart disease can also benefit our skin. When the arteries become clogged from an excess of fat in our diets, all the tissues of the body, including the skin, receive less blood, oxygen, and nutrients. Highly saturated fats also generate more free radicals. The end result is that all parts of the body, including the skin, incur more damage.

2. STOCK UP ON ANTIOXIDANTS

Any foods with antioxidants, such as vitamins C and E, lycopene, green tea extract, etc., are considered to have heart-healthy and even cancer-fighting benefits. Bonus? Many of them destroy the free radicals that eat away at our skin's building blocks, collagen and elastin. Vitamin C actually stimulates collagen production. A diet rich in bright multicolored vegetables and fruits will go far to ensure you are getting enough of these great defenders on a daily basis.

3. EAT EVERYTHING—IN MODERATION, OF COURSE

Diets that advise you to cut out entire food groups will make you miss out on the nutrients necessary for overall health and fabulous-looking skin. For example, extremely low-carbohydrate plans limit fruits and some vegetables—the main sources of antioxidants. Very low-fat diets may be missing essential fatty acids, which the body and skin require to absorb the fat-soluble vitamins, maintain lubrication/moisturization, and repair tissue. Diets must contain protein—one of the essential building blocks for healthy hair, skin, and nails. Calcium, which may not be directly involved with the skin, is extremely important for healthy bone and teeth.

4. CHEW AND SWALLOW

It's better to try to get your nutrients from food rather than from supplements. An overwhelming majority of the nutritional community is now realizing that it's not only the vitamin or mineral in a food that is beneficial, but also the other aspects of the food itself (referred to as the bioavailability) that work synergistically to enhance the vitamin's performance. In addition, while it's extremely difficult to overdose on nutrients from foods, it is possible to have an excessive amount of a vitamin or mineral if you take supplements. It is especially important to avoid an excess of fat-soluble vitamins such as A, E, and D, niacin, B_6, and pantothenic acid, and minerals such as copper, magnesium, and zinc. An excessive amount of some of these supplements can be hazardous to our health.

Caren suggests that if you eat a lot of fortified foods, such as cereals, energy bars, juices, and shakes, check their labels for the amounts of all nutrients before you start taking a vitamin or mineral supplement.

5. DRINK WATER

Not drinking enough water causes dehydration of both the skin and body. This makes our complexion look less firm, radiant, and plump. In my experience, our individual needs for water vary, based on our diet, salt intake, exercise habits, the amount we perspire, and if we live in a hot climate. Our thirst is our body's way of signaling that it needs more water. So let thirst be your guide as to how much water you, specifically, need. If you drink enough water to satisfy your thirst, it will keep your body sufficiently hydrated. If you drink more than that, it probably won't hurt you but it won't make your skin look any better because we just eliminate the excess.

6. DRINK ALCOHOL MODERATELY

While some research indicates that moderate amounts of liquor can benefit the heart, *excessive* drinking just isn't healthy. We've all had too much to drink and awakened the next morning looking and feeling bad. Here's why. Alcohol is a diuretic, so it dehydrates both our skin and our bodies—one of the reasons for that pounding headache the morning after. Dehydrated skin loses its plump, firm, and dewy appearance so it may appear drawn, lax, and more lined than usual. We might also appear puffier, since alcohol is a vasodilator—meaning it opens blood vessels. So while we are trying to sleep off the effects of too many martinis, the alcohol-dilated capillaries leak circulatory fluids into our tissues, causing the skin to swell. The good news? Rehydration (drinking water) revives skin and helps that headache. And as we start moving around throughout the day, our blood flow becomes normalized and our puffiness, along with dark circles will fade.

Too many cocktails disrupt sleep and stimulate free-radical production. Our bodies have to divert blood flow, oxygen, and nutrients away from the skin to our vital organs to help process the alcohol. This action has an additional impact on skin because when skin has poor circulation, it actually creates extra blood vessels to try to get what it needs. This is the reason many alcoholics have so-called gin blossoms—a profusion of broken capillaries on the nose. Last, but not least, alcohol is also taxing to the liver, which is the organ that helps us eliminate toxins. Sallowness is a direct result of a liver having difficulty with its detoxifying duties. The more we drink, the more it stresses our liver. Eventually, it will have less of an ability to eliminate toxins and free radicals from the body and pallor can result. In addition, alcohol actually promotes the growth of "bad collagen," or scar tissue, in both the skin and liver. Cirrhosis is the result of scar tissue developing in the liver, due to the constant onslaught of free radicals.

6. CUT DOWN ON CAFFEINE

Believe it or not, caffeine actually affects the body in many of the same ways alcohol does. Excess caffeine can cause dehydration, disrupt sleep, trigger stress hormones, and because it engorges veins, it can also cause broken capillaries. We know when we've had too much! It can make us jittery, elevate our heart rate, and cause insomnia. Another surefire sign of too much caffeine is dark under-eye circles. Our skin and health would benefit greatly if we limited our caffeine consumption to only one or two cups of coffee a day.

Nutrition for Your Skin

While new ingredients that can beautify your skin and benefit your overall health are being discovered on almost a daily basis, here are some of the important tried and true components of a beauty diet. I've also included a few new ones that have exciting research behind them that should be considered daily essentials.

AMINO ACIDS

What they are: The building blocks of all proteins in our tissues, including skin. There are nine essential amino acids that we need to get from food; the body can make the other eleven.

Where you can find them: Meat, fish, poultry, eggs, dairy products, and beans.

USRDA: None.

ANTHOCYANINS

What they are: Potent antioxidants found in a water-soluble pigment that gives plants brilliant colors ranging from pink through scarlet, purple, and blue.

What they do: Anthocyanins are considered to be helpful in treating and preventing certain types of cancers and heart disease. They also have been found to improve visual acuity, treat circulatory disorders, help diabetes and ulcers, and have antiviral and antimicrobial abilities. Promotes skin health.

Where you can find them: Blueberries, cherries, elderberries, grapes, black currents, and hibiscus flowers.

USRDA: None yet established.

BIOFLAVANOIDS

What they are: Bioflavanoids are another type of plant pigment that keeps fruits and vegetables brightly colored because their potent antioxidant powers prevent the oxidization that turns fruits and vegetables brown. They continue to act as powerful antioxidants in the body. This is one of the reasons multicolored salads and a varied diet of fresh fruits and vegetables are so highly recommended for maintaining optimal health.

What they do: Bioflavanoids are considered by some scientific circles to be more powerful free radical scavengers than vitamins C and E. They are also essential for the stability and absorption of antioxidant vitamin C, one of the key collagen-building catalysts. As with other antioxidants, a high bioflavanoid intake is related to a lower risk of heart attack, cardiovascular disease, and some forms of cancer. Sometimes called flavones or vitamin P because of their effect on the permeability (the rate at which something passes through the cell membranes) of capillaries. Bioflavanoids also have been shown to help heal wounds and support a healthy immune system. They also have antiviral, anti-inflammatory, and antiallergy properties.

Where you can find them: While precise amounts of bioflavanoids in foods have not yet been determined, this type of antioxidant is abundant in apricots, cherries, cantaloupe, papaya, grape seed extract, pine bark extract, citrus fruits, black tea, onions, parsley, legumes, red wine, red grapes, red cabbage, buckwheat, and all blue and purple berries.

USRDA: None yet established.

COENZYME Q-10 (UBIQUINONE, UBIQUINOLE)

What it is: Coenzyme Q-10 is a compound that is made naturally in our bodies and is used by our cells to produce the energy they need for their growth and maintenance. Coenzyme Q-10 is believed to be essential for generating up to 95 percent of the total energy our bodies require in order to function at optimum levels. It is also an antioxidant with actions very similar to those of vitamin E. Coenzyme Q-10 also stimulates our circulation and immune systems. It is believed to have a powerful antiaging effect, as well.

Where you can find it: Mackerel, salmon, sardines, beef, peanuts, and spinach.

USRDA: None

COPPER

What it does: When taken internally, this mineral has been shown to be a significant factor in both hemoglobin and collagen formation.

Where you can find it: Organ meats, seafood, nuts, seeds, wheat bran cereals, whole grain products, and cocoa products.

USRDA: 900 mcg per day for men and women; 1800 for vegetarians because the body needs a certain amount of zinc in order to absorb copper, and many vegetarians are zinc deficient; zinc is less readily absorbed from nonanimal sources. But the exact opposite is also true—an excess amount of zinc can interfere with copper absorption and cause a deficiency.

How to meet it: The exact copper content of foods has not been precisely calculated yet, but if you eat a well-balanced diet of mostly nonprocessed foods, you should have no problem meeting the USRDA.

ESSENTIAL FATTY ACIDS

What they are: Linolenic/omega-3 fatty acids: (includes alpha-linolenic acids and eicosapentaenoic acid (EPA) and linoleic acid/omega-6 fatty acids: (includes linoleic and gamma-linolenic acids). These two polyunsaturated fatty acids are crucial to our body's basic functioning. Since they cannot be made from other substances within the body or from each other, we have to get them from food or supplements.

What they do: Both are components of hormone-like substances that regulate a variety of our bodily functions, including our blood pressure, blood clot formation, and immune response. They are also part of the structure of cell membranes and are essential for rebuilding cells as well as reproducing new ones. Some studies have shown that essential fatty acids (EFAs) also maintain and improve the health of our hair and skin and help to ease eczema and psoriasis. EFAs are also thought to lower cholesterol and triglyceride levels and thus are beneficial to treating and preventing cardiovascular disease.

Where you can find them: Linoleic acid/omega-6 fatty acids (includes linoleic and gamma-linolenic acids) are in oils such as grape seed, evening primrose, sesame, and soybean; seeds; nuts; legumes; and whole grain products. Linolenic/Omega-3 fatty acids (includes alpha-linolenic acids and eicosapentaenoic acid (EPA) are in fresh deepwater fish, including salmon, mackerel, herring, sardines; fish oil; and some vegetable oils, such as canola, flaxseed, and walnut oils.

NOTE: Cooking with these oils actually destroys their EFA content and creates free radicals. It's best to consume them as uncooked liquids (as in salad dressing) or in supplements. It is far healthier to cook foods in olive, safflower, and corn oils.

USRDA: While there is no USRDA for EFAs, experts recommend that they represent 10 to 20 percent of our total daily caloric intake. Many nutritionists offer the following advice to help us meet our EFA needs: Eat fish two to three times per week, as well as a small amount of vegetable oils, to obtain the right balance between omega-6 and omega-3 intakes. The ratio of omega-3 to omega-6 should be about 1 to 4. This ratio is believed by some to be the key to their effectiveness.

GREEN TEA

What it is: A beverage widely consumed in Japan, China, and other Asian nations that has recently gained more widespread popularity in the West. Its main claim to fame is that it is rich in chemicals known as polyphenols (also found in white tea), which have potent antioxidant properties.

What it does: Many researchers believe green tea may help to prevent some cancers because of its high antioxidant content. This theory is largely due to the fact that people in Asian countries who drink green tea seem to have fewer incidences of certain types of cancer, such as prostate, stomach, and esophageal. Also, green tea contains epigallocatechin-3-gallate (EGCG), a compound that is believed to block production of the enzyme required for cancer cells to grow. EGCG may work by suppressing the formation of blood vessels, a process called angiogenesis, thereby cutting off the supply of blood to cancer cells. But while animal studies have been promising, results from human studies have been mixed. Stay tuned.

Meanwhile, favorable research has demonstrated that green tea extract not only can fight both environmental and metabolic free radicals but that it also repairs DNA. Damaged DNA promotes aging, reduces your defenses against free radicals, diminishes your cells' regenerative ability, and can even result in skin cancer.

Green tea may also have numerous other health benefits. Herbalists prescribe it for stomach problems, to reduce tooth decay, to reduce high blood pressure and cholesterol levels, and to help promote healthy circulation by helping shrink blockages of the blood vessels in the heart that can lead to heart attacks.

Where you can find it: In green tea leaves and tea bags.

USRDA: None. But in Asian countries people generally drink three cups a day or more.

IRON

What it does: This mineral is a key component of hemoglobin in our blood and myoglobin (a red protein that comprises our muscles), both of which supply oxygen to cells. A deficiency in iron can lead to anemia, which can cause unduly pale skin, weakness, headaches, reduced resistance to infection, decreased tolerance to cold, and poor circulation, which can rob your skin of the oxygen and nutrients it needs to look its best.

Where you can find it: Red meat, fish, poultry, shellfish, eggs, legumes, and dried fruits.

USRDA: 18 mg per day for menstruating women, 8 mg per day for nonmenstruating women and men. Vegetarians often don't incorporate enough iron into their diets even unwittingly since the body doesn't as easily absorb plant sources of iron. But non-vegetarians should try and eat both animal and plant-based sources of iron for a healthier, better-rounded diet.

How to meet it: ¾ cup of breaded and fried clams, 3.0 mg; 3 oz. dark meat turkey, 2 mg; 3 oz. chicken breast, 1mg; 3 oz. beef tenderloin, 3 mg; 3 oz. roasted white meat turkey, 1.2 mg; 3 oz. blue fin tuna, 1.1mg; ¾ cup 100 percent fortified cereal, 18mg; 1 cup cooked lentils, 6 mg; ½ cup cooked spinach, 3.2 mg; 1 cup cooked kidney beans, 5.2 mg; ½ cup firm tofu, 1.8 mg.

LYCOPENE

What it is: An organic chemical compound that gives yellow, red, or orange plants their color (caretenoid) and is loaded with antioxidants.

What it does: Major studies have found that it prevents the oxidation of low-density lipoprotein (LDL) cholesterol. High LDL oxidation is associated with an increased risk of atherosclerosis and coronary heart disease. Ongoing research suggests that lycopene may reduce the risk of prostate cancer as well as cancers of the lung, bladder, cervix, and skin. Other major studies have shown that lycopene is extremely potent at fending off environmental free radicals and so helps to prevent collagen break down. Lycopene may also diminish the damage of free radicals caused specifically from sun. The scientific and medical communities are fairly convinced that the more lycopene is researched, the more healing powers it will turn out to have.

Where you can find it: Fresh tomatoes, tomato sauce, tomato and tomato-based vegetable juices, tomato soup, tomato ketchup, tomato paste, chili sauce, watermelon, pink grapefruit, guava, apricots, and red papaya.

IMPORTANT NOTE: Research shows that our bodies absorb lycopene in tomatoes more efficiently if it is processed into tomato juice, sauce, paste, or ketchup.

USRDA: None. But major studies have shown that a daily consumption of at least 40 mg of lycopene can help you realize its heart healthy and LDL- reducing benefits.

How to meet it: ½ cup spaghetti sauce, 28.7 mg; 1tbsp tomato ketchup, 2.7 mg; 2tbsp tomato paste, 13.8 mg; 1 slice watermelon, 14.7 mg; ½ pink grapefruit, 4.9 mg; 1 raw tomato, 3.7 mg.

MAGNESIUM

What it does: This mineral activates all our enzymatic systems, which are the catalysts for all our bodily functions. It plays a role in our nerve and muscle functions, is a key component of bone growth, and directly affects our body's ability to metabolize calcium, potassium, and vitamin D. Because magnesium is necessary for the release of cellular energy in all of our body's soft tissues, it has a direct effect on the health of our skin. It also has been found to improve circulation, which also favorably impacts skin. Recent promising studies also have shown that magnesium supplements enable heart disease patients to exercise for longer periods of time. It appears to protect their hearts from the stress of working out.

Where you can find it: Green leafy vegetables; unpolished grains, such as brown rice, wheat germ, and wheat bran; nuts, including almonds and peanuts; meat; milk.

USRDA: 320 mg per day for women; 420 mg per day for men.

How to meet it: 1 oz. of sunflower seeds, 100 mg; 1 oz. almonds, 85 mg; 1 oz. cashews, 75 mg; 1 oz. wheat germ, 70 mg; 1 oz. Brazil nuts, 65 mg; 1 oz. dark chocolate, 35 mg; ½ cup cooked spinach, Swiss chard, or cooked beans, 60 to 80 mg; 3 oz. of most kinds of fish, 50–90 mg.

P. EMBLICA

What it is: An herb derived from the bark, leaves, flowers, and roots of the Phyllanthus emblica tree. It is used in seventeen countries and nations worldwide, including India and Cambodia, for many different medical treatments.

What it does: The bark is a rich source of ellagic acid, another antioxidant that has been shown in some exciting studies to be an anticarcinogen. The fruit is a rich source of antioxidant vitamin C. Oral preparations using some form of P. emblica traditionally have been used to prevent and treat hepatitis, certain forms of cancer, and to strengthen the immune system.

Where to get it: To date, P. emblica isn't widely available, though it may be prescribed orally by some Ayurvedic medical practitioners. Stay tuned.

USRDA: None yet established.

SELENIUM

What it does: In the last ten years, scientists have discovered that this mineral, which works in tandem with vitamin E as an antioxidant, may play a role in preventing cancer, heart disease, and some strains of flu. It seems to keep our tissues (including our skin) elastic and prevent them from hardening due to oxidation (free radical damage). For this reason, scientists are optimistic that selenium is a key component in slowing down the aging process. Recent animal studies also have shown that either when taken orally or applied topically in the form of L-selenomethionine, selenium protects us against both daily incidental and excessive sun damage. Its other health benefits may include playing a role in thyroid function, which regulates the metabolism. And a healthy metabolism equals healthy skin.

Where you can find it: Selenium is readily available in nonprocessed foods, including meats; shellfish; garlic; vegetables; grains, such as oats grown on selenium-rich soil; and Brazil nuts.

USRDA: 55 mcg per day for women; 70 mcg per day for men.

How to meet it: While the nutritional community hasn't yet calculated the precise selenium values in specific foods, it is considered to be one of the easier nutrients to get enough of since it is so widespread.

SOY

What it is: A legume native to Asia that's extensively cultivated for a variety of different food sources.

What it does: Some studies have associated soy with a lower risk for developing heart disease and lower incidences of cancers of the breast, colon, uterus, and prostate. Other studies have used soy to lower cholesterol levels, treat hot flashes, and increase bone density during and after menopause. These reported benefits might have something to do with certain "magical" compounds called isoflavones, also known as phytoestrogens. Phytoestrogens are, in essence, plant estrogens and have some of the same positive effects on the body as natural human or man-made estrogen without some of the negative effects.

Soy's effects on skin have been found to be extremely beneficial in promising and exciting research from Switzerland's Dr. Genistein, who appears to have isolated one of the key isoflavones for skin health. Studies throughout Europe have shown that genistein helps to suppress our body's enzymes that erode collagen. It also appears to react with our skin's estrogen receptors like actual estrogen without any of the negative side effects of hormone replacement therapy (HRT). Several new studies have shown that our collagen-producing fibroblasts have estrogen receptors in them, which would make estrogen an important part of collagen synthesis.

Where you can find it: Soybean, edamame, tofu, tempeh, soy milk, and prepared foods such as soy burgers, soy chips, and veggie burgers.

USRDA: None yet established, though The American Heart Association recently concluded that 25 to 50 grams of soy a day can help lower levels of LDL, or bad cholesterol, by as much as 8 percent.

IMPORTANT NOTE: Some important studies, including one published in the *Journal of Cancer Research*, concluded that eating isoflavone-enhanced supplements containing genistein may counteract the tumor-fighting effects of Tamoxifen, a commonly prescribed medication for women battling estrogen-dependent breast cancer. It has been theorized in an important study that one possible explanation for these findings is the fact that our soy supplements and fortified foods may contain too many isoflavones. In Asia where cancer rates are lower, people often consume diets rich in soy products that contain about 20 to 30 milligrams of isoflavones. However, many isoflavone-enhanced drinks and supplements here may contain 30 to 150 milligrams per serving and often two or more servings a day are recommended on the labels. Several organizations are continuing to research soy's possible role in preventing breast and other cancers and/or furthering it in cases of estrogen-dependent breast cancer. If you have cancer, or are genetically predisposed to it, it's best to check with your doctor before taking *any* oral supplements.

SULFUR

What it is: Sulfur is an element that occurs naturally in the body as a component of the amino acids cysteine and methionine, which means it plays an important role in the structure and thickness of almost all our body's proteins (including collagen), antibodies, and enzymes.

What it does: In terms of skin, sulfur has been found to play a major role in maintaining the solid structure of keratin—a key protein in our hair and nails—and the softer, less rigid, keratin that makes up skin. As a key part of chondroitin sulfate, sulfur also has been found to both stimulate the secretion and increase the viscosity of the fluids that condition our joints and skin. In addition it helps fend off the body's enzymes that break down joints. It also has a powerful anti-inflammatory action on connective tissue disease as well as the ability to regulate immune response. For these reasons, according to promising research, it is thought to play a key role in our skin's health, fending off and perhaps even reversing the signs of premature aging, though more studies are necessary to confirm these findings.

Where you can find it: The major food sources for sulfurs are proteins that contain methionine and cysteine. These include: beans, eggs, beef, pork, and poultry. In addition, unless labeled sulfur-free, dried fruit can be a good source.

USRDA: None. For now, it is assumed that if you eat an adequate amount of protein, you will take in a sufficient amount of sulfur.

VITAMIN A

What it does: In addition to being essential for good vision, as well as healthy bones and teeth, vitamin A, which is fat soluble, is also a powerful antioxidant that may play a role in preventing cancer. It is also key to normal cell development and reproduction and helps to maintain our body's mucous membranes (the linings of the cavities and canals of the body that are exposed to air, such as the inside of the mouth and nose). Vitamin A is also an important component of the development and preservation of our epithelial tissues (the layers of the body that serve as selective barriers to the environment; they include our cornea, skin, respiratory lining, and the lining of the digestive tract). Scientists also believe vitamin A may prevent premature wrinkling and bumpy or sandpaper-like skin. Vitamin A deficiencies can result in rough, dry, scaly, skin.

While more research needs to be done for conclusive evidence, some promising studies also have suggested that when consumed, vitamin A may provide protection against sunburn because of its ability to absorb light. The studies found that moderate amounts of vitamin A (30 mg/day) taken before and during sun exposure gave additional protection against sunburn, possibly because the vitamin A in the body worked synergistically with the physical protection of the sunscreen. It also has been suggested that vitamin A supplements increase skin's reflective abilities, thereby improving its own natural sun protection.

Where you can find it: In nature, vitamin A exists only in its precursor form carotene, a yellow orange pigment that our bodies convert into vitamin A, and beta-carotene, a form of a carotene that our bodies also transform into vitamin A. Carotenes and beta-carotenes are the most abundant in leafy vegetables and dark colored fruits, such as carrots, cantaloupe, sweet potato, butternut squash, spinach, dandelion greens, and turnip greens. They are also present in cow's liver, fish, and dairy products.

USRDA: 700 mcg per day for women; 900 mcg per day for men.

How to meet it: Concentrated sources include: ½ cup cooked carrots, 1915 mcg; ½ cup mashed sweet potato, 1936 mcg; and ½ cup spinach, 737 mcg. Other less concentrated sources include: one cup fortified milk, 140 mcg; and 6 fresh apricots, 560 mcg.

VITAMIN B COMPLEX

What it does: Vitamin B is actually a complex of water-soluble nutrients that work together synergistically. So if you are taking a B vitamin, make sure it contains all nine forms of it to ensure maximum benefits. While each component may have slightly different functions, as a whole, B complex is a coenzyme that is essential in helping the body to metabolize macronutrients, such as fatty and amino acids, and carbohydrates. It also helps maintain the health of the nerves, skin, eyes, hair, liver, and mouth, as well as healthy muscle tone in the gastrointestinal tract and proper brain function.

In terms of skin health, inadequate amounts of vitamin B can lead to rashes (B_2, riboflavin, B_6, and biotin); cracks at the corners of the mouth (B_2, riboflavin); and dry skin, rash, loss of hair, brittle hair and nails (biotin). One component of folic acid, para-aminobenzoic acid (PABA), helps to create pantothenic acid, which is believed to be an antioxidant that helps protect against sunburn and skin cancer. A deficiency of PABA may lead to patchy areas of white skin.

Where you can find it: While each component of vitamin B complex may be found in different foods, whole grains, fortified cereals, green vegetables, red meat, organ meats, dairy, fish, and nuts generally are your richest sources for most of them.

USRDA and how to meet it:

* **B_1 (thiamin):** 1.1 mg per day for women, 1.2 mg per day for men. Some foods that contain it include: a 3.1 oz. broiled pork chop, .33 mg; 1 tablespoon brewer's yeast, 1.25 mg; ¼ cup sunflower seeds, .80 mg; 3 oz. ham .78 mg.

* **B_2 (riboflavin):** 1.1 mg per day for women, 1.3mg per day for men. Some foods that contain it include: 1 cup yogurt, .58 mg; 1 cup cooked mushrooms, .48 mg; 1 cup part-skim ricotta, .46 mg; 1 cup cooked spinach, .42 mg.

* **B_3 (niacin):** 14 mg per day for women, 16 mg per day for men. Some foods that contain it include: 3 oz. tuna packed in water, 10.6 mg; ½ roast chicken breast, 6.2 mg; 1 cup cooked mushrooms, 7 mg, 3 oz. beef liver, 12.2 mg.

* **Folate (folic acid):** 400 mcg per day for men and women, though needs increase to 600 mcg per

day for pregnant women to prevent neural tube defects. Some foods that contain it include: 1 cup black-eyed peas, 350 mcg; 1 cup spinach, 260 mcg; 1 cup pinto beans, 295 mcg, 1 cup asparagus, 175 mcg.

* **B₆ (pyridoxine):** 1.3–1.7 mg per day for men and women. Some foods that contain it: a banana, .6 mcg; 3 oz. sirloin steak, .45 mcg; 3 oz. turkey, .48 mcg; 1 cup spinach, .48 mcg.

* **B₁₂ (cyanocobalmin):** 6 mcg per day for men and women. Some foods that contain it include: 1 cup milk, 2 mcg; ½ oz. cheese, 2 mcg; 1 egg, 2 mcg.

* **Pantothenic acid:** 10 mg per day for men and women. While information concerning exact amounts of pantothenic acid in foods is incomplete, good sources include: chicken, beef, grains, oats, cereal, potatoes, tomatoes, egg yolk, and broccoli.

* **Biotin:** 30 mcg per day for men and women. No one officially has determined the exact amounts of biotin in food but it is definitely present in liver, meats, brewer's yeast, egg yolks, soybeans, saltwater fish, and whole grains.

VITAMIN C (ASCORBIC ACID)

What it does: This proven antioxidant protects our skin and organs from the harmful degenerative effects of free radicals that can cause the cell damage that may contribute to the development of cardiovascular disease, cancer, and other illnesses, as well as premature aging. Vitamin C has also been shown to be necessary for tissue growth and repair, as well as collagen formation. Since it works synergistically with vitamin E, it is recommended that you make sure you get enough of both of these vitamins to receive their maximum benefits.

Where you can find it: Citrus fruits, such as grapefruits, lemons, oranges, and tangerines; other fruits including berries, mangoes, apples, and pineapples; tomatoes; yellow, red, and orange peppers; green vegetables, such as asparagus, avocado, broccoli, kale, and spinach.

USRDA: 75 mg per day for women; 90 mg per day for men.

How you can meet it: It's easy to incorporate enough C into your diet because it's found in concentrated amounts in a lot of different foods. For example, ½ cup of chopped fresh red pepper has 95 mg; 1 cup strawberries, 84 mg; 1 cup orange juice, 93 mg; 1 grapefruit, 94 mg; ½ cup broccoli, 58 mg, and ½ cup brussels sprouts, 48 mg.

VITAMIN D (CALCIFEROL)

What it does: Vitamin D's main claim to fame is that it is essential for the growth of our bones and teeth and for our absorption and utilization of calcium and phosphorous. This function makes it an important nutrient in the treatment and prevention of osteoporosis, a dangerous decrease in bone mass, and the less severe osteopenia. It is also involved in regulating the heartbeat, protecting against muscle weakness, and is essential for normal blood clotting.

When it comes to skin, some clinical studies have shown that vitamin D, which is fat soluble, may help make the symptoms of psoriasis less severe. In addition, vitamin D is involved in maintaining normal thyroid function, which is essential to healthy skin.

Where you can find it: The form of vitamin D we get from food and supplements doesn't become active without the help of our bodies. Then our skin gets into the act. When we go out into the sun, the UV rays transform a cholesterol compound in our skin into the precursor of vitamin D, which is then converted into its active form by our liver and kidneys. Experts have found that exposing our face or arms to the sun for just 15 minutes 3 times a week is a sufficient way to get enough vitamin D. It can also be found in fish liver oils; vegetable oils; fatty saltwater fish, like halibut, salmon, tuna, sardines, and shrimp; dairy products; egg yolks; and dandelion greens.

USRDA: Anywhere from 5 to 15 mcg per day depending on age. Growing children and adolescents require more than adults.

How to meet it: 3 oz. of shrimp, 3 mcg; 2 eggs, 1.3 mcg; 1 cup of milk, 2.5 mcg; 3 oz. of mackerel or salmon, 8 mcg; 3 oz. blue fin tuna, 4 mcg.

VITAMIN E (TOCOPHEROL)

What it does: Vitamin E is a fat-soluble vitamin that actually exists in eight forms, called tocopherols. Each form has its own function in our bodies. Alpha-tocopherol is the most active form for us since it is the most easily absorbed by our bodies. It is another powerful antioxidant that defends us against and disables metabolic free radicals. It also improves our circulation; protects the membranes of our red blood cells; safeguards our white blood cells, which help our bodies fend off disease; plays an important role in our nerve development; and is a necessary component of tissue repair.

Where you can find it: Vegetable oils, including canola, flaxseed, corn, safflower, soybean, and wheat germ; nuts, seeds, and legumes, such as sunflower seeds, walnuts, and soybeans; whole grains and fortified cereals, including brown rice, cornmeal, and oatmeal. There is also a small amount of vitamin E in meat, poultry, fish, and eggs.

USRDA: 15 mg per day of the alpha-tocopherol form for men and women. Unlike other vitamins, the form of alpha-tocopherol made in the laboratory and found in supplements is not identical to the natural form, and isn't quite as active. For this reason, some experts in the medical community are now recommending that we take supplements with mixed tocopherols, such as beta, gamma, and delta along with alpha.

How you can meet it: ½ cup mashed sweet potato has 4.5 mg; 2 tablespoons sunflower seeds, 9 mg; 1 tablespoon canola oil, 2.9 mg.

VITAMIN K

What it does: Vitamin K is essential to blood clotting and the making of a protein in our blood that regulates calcium in our bloodstream. It is also necessary for bone function and repair, and the synthesis of osteocalcin (a protein in bone tissue on which calcium crystallizes) and so may help prevent osteoporosis. Vitamin K heals and prevents broken blood vessels. In fact, symptoms of vitamin K deficiency include easy bruising and ruptured capillaries, a key cause of dark under-eye circles.

Where you can find it: Green veggies, such as collard greens, spinach, salad greens, and broccoli; brussels sprouts; cabbage; plant oils;

garbanzo beans; eggs; milk; beef liver. Small amounts are also found in: tomatoes, lima beans, apricots, potatoes, grapes, cauliflower, peaches, plums and squash.

USRDA: 90 mcg per day for men and women.

How to meet it: Precise levels of the vitamin K content of foods have not yet been determined. But here are some estimates most widely considered to be the most accurate: 3 oz. dark green leafy veggies, 50 to 800 mcg; 3.5 oz. of Swiss chard or kale, 800–830 mcg; 3.5 oz. brussels sprouts or spinach, 400–440 mcg.

IMPORTANT NOTE: Since an excess amount of vitamin K in supplement form can easily reach harmful levels, it is only available as a single dose by prescription. Toxic side effects from excess supplementation may include: breakage of red blood cells and the release of their pigment, which turns skin yellow, and more seriously, brain damage. If you take anticoagulants, your doctor might advise you to avoid or limit the foods that contain vitamin K, due to its clotting effects.

WHITE TEA

What it is: A specific form of tea, mostly grown in China, in which the leaves and buds are simply steamed and dried, rather than undergoing the withering and various degrees of oxidation that black, oolong, and green teas are processed with.

What it does: Studies have shown that white tea may be extremely effective in fending off DNA mutations and certain forms of cancers due to its high polyphenol content, which has been found to be an effective weapon against free radical damage. Many researchers believe white tea is so high in antioxidants because it undergoes minimal processing and so is able to maintain its protective powers. White tea has also been found to protect the skin's lipid content, both when applied topically and taken internally.

Where you can find it: In silver-tip white tea leaves and tea bags.

USRDA: None so far. But again, people in Asian cultures tend to drink several cups of white tea on a daily basis.

The Next Wave in Antioxidants

Four Extremely Promising New Comers

Much remains to be learned about the following antioxidants to confirm the exact nature of their actions and their effects on our bodies: anthocyanins, bioflavanoids, lycopene, and P. emblica. The content in food of many of these antioxidants are still unknown, which makes accurate estimates for our consumption of them and the correlation with their benefits difficult. And though we do have more complete data on lycopene, the effects of processing and cooking bioflavanoids, anthocyanins, and P. emblica, are not completely realized. We also aren't completely sure how these antioxidants are absorbed into the bloodstream. But in general, the scientific and medical communities are highly optimistic that more research will help back up the health claims of existing studies. Applying them topically is a safe and effective way for the skin to benefit from them.

ZINC

What it does: This mineral is essential for our normal growth and development and the functioning of our immune system and reproductive organs. It also plays a significant part in our night vision and sense of taste. In addition, zinc is a key nutrient in helping to maintain the health of our skin, hair, and bones. Some studies have also found that zinc links together the amino acids that are necessary for collagen formation and essential to healing wounds. It has also been shown to help prevent damage to our skin's collagen and elastin fibers.

Where you can find it: Meat, shellfish, and poultry are the most concentrated sources of zinc. Plant sources include some legumes, soybeans, and whole grains, but our bodies do not as easily absorb them.

USRDA: 8 mg per day for women; 11 mg per day for men.

How to meet it: 6 medium battered and fried oysters, 16 mg; 3-oz. pork shoulder, 4.8 mg; 3 oz. beef tenderloin, 4.8 mg; 3 oz. pork tenderloin, 2.5 mg; ¾ cup ready-to-eat breakfast cereal, fortified with 100 percent of the USRDA for zinc per serving, 15.0 mg; 1 cup plain low-fat yogurt, 2.2 mg; ½ cup baked beans, 1.7 mg; 1 oz. dry roasted, unsalted cashews, 1.6 mg.

Active Ingredients Checklist

THE ESSENTIALS FOR AN EFFECTIVE DAILY ANTIAGING REGIMEN

We've covered a lot of ground in the previous pages and while getting and maintaining young and beautiful skin may seem complicated, it's actually quite simple. The cornerstone is a solid daily regimen that in addition to appropriate cleansing and moisturizing includes products with proven active ingredients that:

* Protect against the sun, free radicals, and our collagen-degrading enzymes.
* Speed up cell turnover to keep skin clear, smooth, and evenly toned.
* Build collagen and elastin to stave off lines, wrinkles, and sagging and to minimize their appearance.

The ingredients that achieve those results are available in varying forms (e.g., creams, lotions, gels, serums, and pads), at different locations (e.g., your local drugstore, department store, specialty boutique, online, at your dermatologist's office), and at varying price points. The main thing is to pick formulations geared to your skin type that are pleasant to use with a price tag that you are comfortable with. Remember, higher prices don't necessarily mean more efficacious products, though they generally do mean a product with more medical-grade ingredients.

Look for skin-care therapies that contain muliple active ingredients. These products are usually more effective than products that only contain one active ingredient because they take a multi-faceted approach to treating the skin.

You might find that it's necessary to fine-tune your regimen depending on the season, and if you are traveling or taking any medications, these factors can affect your skin balance to promote irritation and inflammation, which can accelerate the aging process by producing free radicals. Products that cause up to three minutes of tingling, not burning, are fine but more than that may be a sign of irritation. (Reread chapter 4 to review how.) But if a product burns, causes itching, flaking, or redness, stop using it immediately. Similarly, if you are not seeing some kind of positive results after four to six weeks, it's time to move on. With all of this in mind, here is your cheat sheet of essential antiaging actions and their corresponding ingredients that should be used daily:

PROTECTION

Sun

Look for products that offer broad spectrum UVA/UVB protection geared for your skin type with a minimum of SPF 15.

Free Radical

Proven antioxidants to fight free radicals include vitamins C and E. Up and coming ingredients with promising research behind them are:

* Lycopene, found in tomatoes, watermelon, red grapes, and pomegranate
* Green tea extract
* White tea extract
* Grapeseed extract
* Beta-Carotene, a provitamin A, found in carrots, and dark leafy greens
* Bioflavanoids, found in blueberries and raspberries
* Anthocyanins, found in red grapes
* P. emblica extracts from the fruit, bark, and/or leaves of the Phyllanthus emblica tree.

Collagen Erosion:

* Retinoids: Nonprescription strength retinol; prescription strength tretinoins used in Retin-A and Renova
* Genistein: a component of soy extract.

SPEED UP CELL TURNOVER THROUGH EXFOLIATION

* Alpha Hydroxy Acids: A class of acids that occur naturally in foods. These include:

Glycolic: from sugar
Lactic: from milk
Citric: from citrus fruits
Malic: from apples

* Beta Hydroxy Acids: Currently, Salicylic Acid is the only beta hydroxy acid used in skin care. While it's synthetic, it is close to the molecular structure to an acid that occurs naturally in skin, so it is generally nonirritating.

BUILD COLLAGEN AND ELASTIN STORES WITH

* Vitamin C
* Vitamin A-derived retinoids: Nonprescription strength retinol; prescription strength, tretinoins
* Genistein: This soy derivative works like estrogen without negative side effects to prompt the skin's collagen-producing fibroblasts to get moving.

OPTIONAL PROBLEM SOLVERS

Lighten Dark Spots with:

Bleaching Agents:

* Kojic Acid: Available in both prescription and nonprescription strength
* Hydroquinone: Available in both prescription and nonprescription strength
* Vitamin C in the form of ascorbic acid
* Vitamin K: To heal broken capillaries to help prevent them from leaking iron and blood cells in the under-eye area, which gives it a dark appearance.

Deflate Puffy Under-Eyes with:

Natural Diuretics:
* Cucumber extract
* Caffeine

Anti-irritants
* Green tea extract
* White tea extract

RESOURCE LIST

This compiled list of resources can answer any questions you may have after reading this book, or about other products, procedures, or health information you've heard about.

For more information on Dr. Gross, his practice, and the M.D. Skincare line:

M.D. Skincare
444 Madison Ave
8th Floor
New York, NY 10022
Phone: 1-888-830-SKIN (1-888-830-7546)
wwd.mdskincare.com
www.drdennisgross.com

To check the board certification status of a dermatologist:

The American Board of Dermatology

American Board of Dermatology
Henry Ford Health System
1 Ford Place
Detroit, Michigan 48202-3450
Phone: 313-874-1088
Fax: 313-872-3221
www.abderm.org
E-mail: abderm@hfhs.org

For more information on skin concerns and procedures:

The American Academy of Dermatology

P.O. Box 4014
Schaumburg, IL 60168-4014
Phone: 847-330-0230
Fax: 847-330-0050
www.aad.org

The American Academy of Dermatology cannot answer medical questions, give referrals to specific dermatologists, or endorse products.

To contact the AAD for more information about locating a dermatologist, call 888-462-DERM (888-462-3376):

American Society for Dermatologic Surgery

5550 Meadowbrook Dr.
Suite 120
Rolling Meadows, IL 60008

Phone: 847-956-0900
Fax: 847-956-0999
www.asds-net.org
E-mail: info@asds.net

To check the board certification status of a plastic surgeon:

The American Board of Plastic Surgery
Seven Penn Center, Suite 400
1635 Market Street
Philadelphia, PA 19103-2204
Phone: 215-587-9322
Fax: 215-587-9622
abplsurg.org
E-mail: info@abplsurg.org

For more information on plastic surgery procedures and/or to find a board certified plastic surgeon in your area:

American Society of Plastic Surgeons
Plastic Surgery Educational Foundation
444 E. Algonquin Rd.
Arlington Heights, IL 60005
Plastic Surgeon Referral Service: 1-888-4-PLASTIC (1-888-475-2784)
www.plasticsurgery.org

The American Society for Aesthetic Plastic Surgery
Raleigh, North Carolina 27607-7506
Phone: 919-881-2570
Fax: 919-881-2575
Find a surgeon and cost information: 1-888-ASAPS-11 (1-888-272-7711)
www.surgery.org
E-mail: findasurgeon@surgery.org

To check the board certification status of an anesthesiologist:

American Board of Anesthesiology
You may check board status free of charge by:

* Using the *Online Diplomate Directory*
* Calling the ABA at 919-881-2570
* Calling the American Board of Medical Specialties toll free at 866-ASK-ABMS (866-275-2267)

www.abanes.org
The board does not accept correspondence via e-mail.

For more information on health care and concerns:

The National Library of Medical Concerns
Bethesda, MD 20894
Phone: 888-FIND-NLM (888-346-3656)
Fax: 888-346-3656
http://www.nlm.nih.gov

For more information on the safety and efficacy of skin-care products and procedures:

Food and Drug Administration
5600 Fishers Lane
Rockville, MD 20857
1-888-INFO-FDA (1-888-463-6332)
http://www.fda.gov

For more information on alternative and holistic medical procedures, products, and nutrition:

**The National Center for Complementary
and Alternative Medicine**
NCCAM Clearinghouse
P.O. Box 7923
Gaithersburg, MD 20898
Phone: 888-644-6226
International: 301-519-3153
TTY:1-866-464-3615 (for hearing impaired)
Fax: 1-866-464-3616
www.nccam.nih.gov
E-mail: info@nccam.nih.gov

For more information on food and nutrition:

**The Food and Nutrition Information Center
at the National Agricultural Library**
Agricultural Research Service, USDA
National Agricultural Library, Room 105

10301 Baltimore Avenue
Beltsville, MD 20705-2351
Phone: 301-504-5719
Fax: 301-504-6409
TTY: 301-504-6856
www.nal.usda.gov/fnic
E-mail: fnic@nal.usda.gov

NUTRITION.GOV

www.nutrition.gov

INDEX